PERENNIALS

RICHARD ROSENF

A DORLING KINDERSLEY BOOK

**LONDON, NEW YORK,
MUNICH, MELBOURNE, DELHI**

Series Editor Zia Allaway
Series Art Editor Alison Donovan
Managing Editor Anna Kruger
Managing Art Editor Lee Griffiths
Consultant Louise Abbott
DTP Designer Louise Waller
Media Resources Richard Dabb, Lucy Claxton
Picture Research Bridget Tily
Production Controller Mandy Inness

Produced on behalf of Dorling Kindersley by
HILTON/SADLER
Editorial director: Jonathan Hilton
Design director: Peggy Sadler

Introduction Text Zia Allaway

First published in Great Britain in 2003 by
Dorling Kindersley Limited
80 Strand, London, WC2R ORL
A Penguin company

A CIP catalogue record for this book is available
from The British Library
ISBN 0 7513 3823 0

Colour reproduction by Colourscan, Singapore
Printed and bound by Printer Trento, Italy

see our complete catalogue at
www.dk.com

Gardening with perennials

For a garden overflowing with flowers and foliage from spring, through summer to autumn, plant it with perennials. Feathery ferns, free-flowering cranesbills and tall, spiky phormiums all fall within this group, their exquisite beauty and reliability combining to make them among the most popular of all garden plants. Most perennials are easy to look after, too, popping up year after year to adorn beds, borders, and containers. Their versatility and variety of flower and form makes an invaluable contribution to any design, from a traditional cottage garden to modern minimalist roof terrace.

To understand how to use perennials in your garden, it's helpful to know how they grow. A perennial is a plant that lives for more than three years and produces herbaceous, or soft, growth which doesn't become woody like the stems of shrubs and trees. Most perennials die down in winter and the top growth reappears the following spring. Although this factor must be considered when creating a garden where interest is required all year round, with careful planning, you can include evergreen perennials and those that flower very early and late in the year to keep the show going.

◀ **Electric blue corydalis** brightens up borders from early spring to summer.

▶ **Easy to grow and free flowering**, cranesbills offer great value for money.

Naturalistic planting styles

The beauty of perennials is that they suit all gardens, large and small, and can be used in many different designs. For a romantic cottage garden, select a medley of colours and forms, and try mixing perennials with annuals and shrub roses to create flower-filled borders that have a random, naturalistic look. Excellent choices for this style include poppies, daisy-like coreopsis, lupins and tall delphiniums.

Another natural gardening design style, known as 'Prairie planting', uses perennials to mimic the way plants grow in the wild. A limited number of species is planted in large informal swathes, with one variety blending seamlessly into the next, creating waves of colour and texture.

Prairie planting also relies heavily on grasses, such as *Miscanthus sinensis* and *Calamagrostis*, which soften the contours of the planting and, when left to stand over winter, their dried stems and flower spikes provide structure after

A dusting of frost on faded sedum flowers offers late autumn interest.

Waves of colour and form are created in a prairie garden, which combines grasses and perennials.

other perennials have died down. Breaking with formal gardening convention, tall 'see-through' plants, such as *Verbena bonariensis*, with its slim stems topped by buttons of purple flowers, are often planted in front of shorter plants. This blurs the focus and gives prairie-style gardens an almost dream-like quality.

Diminutive evergreen grasses planted in clay pots contrast well with summer perennials, such as hostas.

Formal gardens

Perennials look wonderful when used in wild and natural gardens, but they're equally effective in formal spaces. The hard lines of a geometric lawn or paved area are softened beautifully when edged with flowing borders filled with perennials. When creating formal borders, a simple planting plan and limited palette of colours will produce the most elegant designs. A garden filled with just white or blue plants is a classic example of a formal scheme, although even bright pinks or oranges work well when used in moderation and offset by cooler tones.

Modern spaces

Contemporary gardens can be enriched with perennials, too. Sculptural shrubs form the foundations of many modern designs, but the

Perennials look at home in a traditional garden, while large swathes of plants offer a modern twist.

subtle shapes and colours of perennials also work extremely well as foils for modern building materials, such as concrete and steel. A long border of catmint (*Nepeta sibirica*) when set against a simple rendered wall, for example, will inject texture and colour, while creating an evolving shadow display as the sun moves across the sky. Tall, elegant irises are another option, offering distinctive flowers in early summer and architectural foliage over a long period.

This book includes some of the best and most reliable perennials to help you to design your garden beds and borders. Use it for research or as a quick reference to take with you to the nursery or garden centre.

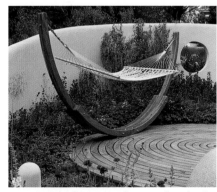

Contemporary features, such as smooth rendered walls, provide a perfect foil for soft, informal perennials.

Choosing perennials

WITH SO MANY PERENNIALS to choose from, it's easy to find one that suits the site and soil in your garden and fits the style and planting scheme. Before buying, always check over the plant for signs of disease or poor growth, and only select healthy specimens. The checklist below will help you to make a good choice.

Strong, healthy top-growth

Disease-free, vigorous leaves

Moist compost, free of weeds and moss

Established, vigorous roots

Pot-bound roots

Before buying a plant, check that its roots have not become constricted or pot-bound. This will cause poor growth, as it limits a plant's ability to take in nutrients and water.

Planting perennials

The beauty of container-grown perennials is that they can be planted at any time of the year, as long as the soil is not frozen or waterlogged, although the best times are spring and autumn. In autumn, the soil tends to be wet and warm, enabling perennials to establish roots quickly before the onset of winter. In cold areas, spring planting is best for perennials that do not like cold, wet conditions. Planting in drier summer months requires more aftercare, and you will need to water your plants well for a few weeks or months until they are established. Before planting, ensure your soil is weed free.

1 Preparing the planting hole

Water the plant thoroughly before planting. Dig a hole 1½ times wider and a little deeper than the root ball. Then water the hole and allow it to drain. Holding the stems between your fingers, tip the plant out of its pot.

2 Teasing out the roots

Mix the removed soil with some well-rotted compost, and add some more compost to the bottom of the planting hole. If the roots are coiled around the sides of the pot, tease them out very carefully.

3 Planting and finishing off

Place the plant in the hole with its crown at the correct depth, which is usually the same as it was in its pot (see overleaf). Gradually backfill around the plant with the mix of soil and compost, firming gently as you go.

Planting depths

To get your plants off to a good start, ensure that they are planted at the correct depth. The majority should be planted at the same level as they were in their pots, but some prefer their crowns (where the stems meet the roots) to sit in the damp soil below the surface. Others will rot unless their crowns are set above the soil.

Crown level with soil surface

Crown 2.5cm (1in) below the soil level

Crown proud of ground level

Crown 10cm (4in) below the soil

Ground level planting

Most perennials, including this Michaelmas daisy, are planted at ground level. This means that the crown is level with the soil surface, as it would have been in its original pot.

Shallow planting

Shallow planting is best for perennials that need moist soil, such as this hosta. Shallow plant by positioning the crown 2.5cm (1in) below the surface of the soil.

Deep planting

Perennials with tuberous root systems, such as this polygonatum, often need to be planted deeply. Set the crown at about 10cm (4in) below the surface of the soil for good results.

Raised planting

Perennials that are prone to rotting at the base, or have variegated foliage that may revert to green, like this sisyrinchium, are planted with the crown just above ground level.

Looking after perennials

PERENNIALS ARE GENERALLY low-maintenance plants. Once established, they only need to be watered during dry periods and adjacent weeds removed promptly. If you also apply an organic mulch, such as well-rotted compost, over the soil, these jobs become even easier. A mulch suppresses weeds, keeps moisture in the soil and slowly releases nutrients. This just leaves you to pick off the fading blooms.

Watering perennials

Water newly planted perennials regularly, even those that like dry soil. Once the roots are well developed, watering regimes vary, depending on the plant and soil.

Improving flowering

Extend the flowering period of your perennials using the following methods. Removing flowers before they set seed stimulates a plant to produce more blooms. Also, for a bushier plant, thin out spindly and weak shoots in spring which will encourage new stems to develop from the base.

Pinching out
When plants reach one-third of their final height, pinch out the stem tips to encourage sideshoots to develop.

Deadheading
Encourage more flowering shoots to develop by removing flowers as soon as they start to fade.

Cutting back
After flowering, when new shoots are visible at the base, cut back the flowered stems to ground level.

Propagating perennials

THERE ARE MANY WAYS to propagate new plants from old. Growing perennials from seed or dividing clumps in spring or autumn are simple methods, although taking stem or root cuttings is also easy. Plants raised from seed may not flower for two years or more.

Growing perennials from seed

It's cheap and easy to grow large numbers of perennials from seed. When collecting the seeds yourself, take them only from strong plants that are free from disease. Sow seeds as soon as they are ripe in summer or autumn, and keep the seedlings in a sheltered place to overwinter.

1 Preparing the seedbed
Fill a clean tray with moist seed compost and firm it gently with a presser to about 1cm (½in) below the rim.

2 Sowing the seed
Use clean, folded paper to sow the seeds evenly and thinly over the surface.

3 Covering the seed
Cover with glass or clear plastic to retain moisture. Place in a cold frame until two pairs of leaves develop.

4 Pricking out
When plants are big enough to handle, transplant them into pots. Take care not to damage the stem or roots.

Dividing perennials

The most common way to increase perennials is by division. This eases overcrowding and by removing weak and unproductive sections also revitalizes older, less vigorous plants. Replant only healthy sections. Perennials are usually divided when dormant, in late autumn or early spring.

1 Lifting clumps
Water the plant before lifting. Then, carefully insert a fork beyond the edge of the clump and lift gently to reduce the risk of root damage. Shake off excess soil.

2 Dividing by hand
Tease apart the roots by hand, keeping healthy sections. Cut back old or dead top-growth. Dig new planting holes, water them, and then replant the divisions.

Alternative methods

Dividing with back-to-back forks
For large, congested clumps of perennials, place two forks back to back, touching where the tines meet the shaft, and lever them apart to divide the root system.

Dividing with a spade
Use a sharp spade to chop through plants with tough, woody roots. For plants that won't divide easily, set the spade in position and stand on it using your full body weight.

A-Z of Perennials

GROWING FROM SEED

Collect fully ripe seeds and sow them at 15°C (59°F). Seedlings take three years to flower. Protect plants from frost during their first winter.

A

Acanthus spinosus Bear's breeches

SHOWY, VERTICAL STEMS with white flowers protruding from purple bracts make this acanthus a striking accent plant. The ground-level leaves, which have spiny edges, are equally architectural and can grow up to 90cm (36in) long. Although tall, it is best to site it toward the front of a border, with space around, so that both flowers and foliage can be seen clearly. Plant it in free-draining but rich soil, and take precautions against attacks from slugs and snails. The huge blooms can be dried for an indoor display, and the seed collected in the autumn for growing new plants.

OTHER VARIETIES *A. dioscoridis* var. *perringii* (shorter-growing, grey-green leaves); *A. hungaricus* (white or pale pink flowers); *A. mollis* (purple-tinted stems); *A. syriacus* (greenish-white flowers).

PLANT PROFILE

HEIGHT 1.5m (5ft)

SPREAD 60cm (24in)

SITE Sun or partial shade

SOIL Fertile, free-draining

HARDINESS Fully hardy

FLOWERING Late spring to midsummer

Achillea filipendulina 'Gold Plate' Yarrow

A

FLAT HEADS OF GOLDEN FLOWERS on strong, erect stems produce a bold display throughout the summer, and combine well with crimson poppies, blue delphiniums, ox eye daisies and hollyhocks. The prolific flowers are good for cutting, lasting well in water without any special treatment, and they can also be dried for use in winter arrangements. Yarrow is easy to grow, tolerating a broad range of soil types. Although the stems are stiff, they tend to bend forward and may need some support. Note that because the foliage can trigger skin allergies, gloves should be worn when handling.

OTHER VARIETIES *A.* 'Lachsschönheit' (pink flowers); *A.* x *lewisii* 'King Edward' (low, mound-forming); *A.* 'Summerwine' (red flowers).

PLANT PROFILE
HEIGHT 1.2m (4ft)
SPREAD 45cm (18in)
SITE Full sun
SOIL Moist, free-draining
HARDINESS Fully hardy
FLOWERING Early summer to early autumn

A | *Aciphylla aurea* Bayonet plant

THIS UNUSUAL PERENNIAL FROM NEW ZEALAND may look far too exotic for cold-climate gardens, but it is actually fully hardy. It makes a large clump of sword-like leaves and the scores of tiny golden-brown flowers (only appearing in long, hot summers) are protected by spiny growths. It needs to be grown in rich, free-draining soil with other architectural plants – if planted in the middle of a typical summer border it can look out of place. The fruit is only produced when there are male and female plants in close proximity.

OTHER VARIETY   *A. scott-thomsonii* (much taller-growing, yellowish-green flowers).

PLANT PROFILE
HEIGHT 1m (3ft)
SPREAD 1m (3ft)
SITE Full sun
SOIL Fertile, free-draining
HARDINESS Fully hardy
FLOWERING Early to late summer

Aconitum carmichaelii 'Arendsii' Monkshood

A

STIFF, VERTICAL FLOWER STEMS with a profusion of deep violet or blue, hood-like flowers held well clear of the dark green leaves make this a contender for cool colour-themed gardens. It also blends well with the white-flowering *Aconitum x cammarum* 'Grandiflorum Album'. Like all monkshoods, 'Arendsii' needs plenty of well-rotted organic matter forked into the soil, especially when grown in full sun, to keep the ground moist; semi-shade is best, however. Note that all parts of the monkshood are highly toxic if ingested, and contact with the skin can lead to an unpleasant irritation.

OTHER VARIETIES *A. x cammarum* 'Bicolor' (blue and white flowers); *A. x carmichaelii* 'Barker's Variety' (deep violet flowers).

PLANT PROFILE
HEIGHT To 1.2m (4ft)
SPREAD 30cm (12in)
SITE Partial shade or full sun
SOIL Moist, fertile
HARDINESS Fully hardy
FLOWERING Early autumn

A

Actaea rubra Red baneberry

FEATHERY, WHITE, EARLY-SUMMER FLOWERS and a profusion of tiny, bright red autumn berries are the big attractions. The best site is a lightly shaded garden where the soil is damp and enriched with plenty of leaf mould. Baneberry can also be grown on banks beside a stream. If growing a couple of plants, include *Actaea alba* with its attractive white berries, each marked with a black spot. Plant all baneberries out of the reach of young children, as the berries are highly toxic if ingested. If you want young plants to fill out a display, divide clumps in early spring, before full growth begins.

OTHER VARIETIES   *A. simplex* 'James Compton' (dark purple foliage, scented cream flowers); *A. spicata* (white flowers, black berries).

PLANT PROFILE
HEIGHT 45cm (18in)
SPREAD 30cm (12in)
SITE Partial shade
SOIL Moist, fertile
HARDINESS Fully hardy
FLOWERING Mid-spring to early summer

Adenophora bulleyana Gland bellflower

A

WITH FLOWERS LIKE THOSE OF A CAMPANULA that appear in clusters on top of tall, thin spikes, this plant is sometimes called the gland bellflower. Use it to inject late–summer colour into the garden, to tower over shorter evergreen shrubs or as part of the build-up to a tall focal point. It can be accommodated in borders where the soil is fertile and moist but free-draining, and can also be grown in wild gardens. Because mature plants dislike being moved, position yours carefully at the outset. In spring, as new growth emerges, look out for slugs and snails which can cause serious damage.

OTHER VARIETIES *A. liliifolia* (shorter-growing, pale blue, fragrant flowers); *A. tashiroi* (branching stems, attractive foliage).

PLANT PROFILE
HEIGHT 1.2m (4ft)
SPREAD 30cm (12in)
SITE Sun or partial shade
SOIL Moist, fertile, free-draining
HARDINESS Fully hardy
FLOWERING Late summer

A | *Aegopodium podagraria* 'Variegatum' Variegated ground elder

THIS IS THE BEST AND ONLY type of ground elder to grow. It is
extremely attractive but, although invasive, is not as thuggish as the
parent plant, *Aegopodium podagraria*. 'Variegatum' has creamy-white
margins and markings on each leaf, and rather insignificant white
flowers. It thrives in the shady parts of the garden and in any type
of soil, including poor ground, making it excellent ground cover.
Few ornamental plants can be grown on poor soil and in shade, and
in these situations it does not pose a threat to other plants. When
planting elsewhere, create a medium-size, walled planting hole,
sealing the sides with old tiles or similar material, to help prevent
the roots from spreading excessively.

PLANT PROFILE	
HEIGHT 30–60cm (12–24in)	
SPREAD Indefinite	
SITE Full or partial shade	
SOIL Average	
HARDINESS Fully hardy	
FLOWERING Early summer	

Dig up and divide large clumps in the spring. Using a clean, sharp knife, trim off all old stems and damaged tissue. Dust the wounds with fungicide to prevent rot, and replant the clumps in the garden.

Agapanthus 'Blue Giant' African lily

A

STARBURSTS OF RICH BLUE FLOWERS held above long sturdy stems make a bold statement in a midsummer border. This African lily also looks dramatic in large tubs positioned on patios, or when planted in groups in gravel gardens, especially when combined with *Agapanthus* 'Bressingham White' with its snow white blooms. Grow these plants in rich, free-draining soil, and ensure they have plenty of moisture during the growing season. Many agapanthus will not suffer low temperatures, but this cultivar is hardier than most, especially when provided with a thick mulch of compost where winters are cold.

OTHER VARIETIES *A. campanulatus* (smaller-growing, greyish-green leaves, sometimes white flowers); *A.* 'Loch Hope' (later-flowering).

PLANT PROFILE

HEIGHT 1.2m (4ft)

SPREAD 60cm (24in)

SITE Full sun

SOIL Moist, fertile, free-draining

HARDINESS Fully hardy

FLOWERING Mid- and late summer

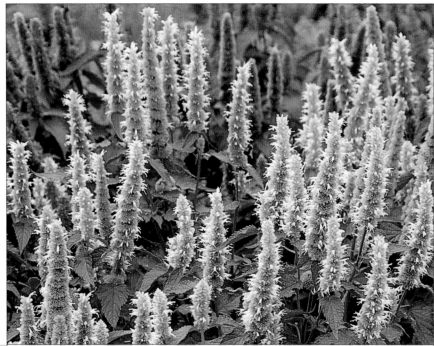

A

Agastache foeniculum 'Alabaster' Anise hyssop

VERTICAL SPIKES OF WHITE FLOWERS make a pleasant backdrop to a pond in summer, although it will not enjoy the moist conditions at the water's edge, preferring free-draining soil. The aniseed-scented leaves are clumped beneath the flowers, offering shade and hiding places for frogs and toads. Not totally hardy, *Agastache foeniculum* needs protection in cold winters and must be planted in a sheltered spot – at the base of a warm wall is ideal – in reasonably fertile soil. Although this hyssop suffers from a reputation of being short-lived, this is not a problem because it self-seeds freely.

OTHER VARIETIES *A. barberi* (red-purple flowers); *A. barberi* 'Firebird' (copper flowers); *A. barberi* 'Tutti-Frutti' (dark pink-red flowers).

PLANT PROFILE
HEIGHT 1m–1.5m (3–5ft)
SPREAD 30cm (12in)
SITE Full sun
SOIL Fertile, free-draining
HARDINESS Frost hardy
FLOWERING Midsummer to early autumn

Ajuga reptans 'Catlin's Giant' Bugle

A

THIS SPREADING EVERGREEN has tall, dark blue flower spikes, but its chief asset is the colourful dark bronze-purple foliage. It prefers moist soil although this particular bugle is tolerant of a wide range of conditions, including poor ground and shade. Avoid deep shade, however, if you want the best foliage colour. 'Multicolor', often sold as 'Rainbow', has equally attractive foliage with bronze-green leaves and unusual cream and pink markings. Of the bugles grown for their flowers, try *Ajuga reptans* 'Purple Torch' which has spikes of lavender-pink flowers. Divide plants in the spring or autumn.

OTHER VARIETIES *A. reptans* (dark-green leaves); *A. reptans* 'Burgundy Glow' (silvery-green leaves suffused with deep wine-red); *A. reptans* 'Pink Elf' (compact with deep pink flowers).

PLANT PROFILE

HEIGHT 15cm (6in)

SPREAD 60–90cm (24–36in)

SITE Partial shade

SOIL Moist

HARDINESS Fully hardy

FLOWERING Late spring and early summer

A

Alchemilla mollis Lady's mantle

THIS INDISPENSABLE GROUND–COVER PLANT self-seeds freely to form clumps of lime-green leaves and sprays of tiny greenish-yellow flowers, and is typically grown at the front edge of a border. To get the most out of it, shear over the plant after its first flush of flowers to promote a second flowering and new leaves. Promptly removing dead flowers also prevents it spreading. Lady's mantle thrives just about anywhere, even in poor soil, and is drought tolerant. Use its foliage to contrast with, for example, purple or blue lavenders.

OTHER VARIETIES *A. alpina* (silver-hairy underside of leaves); *A. ellenbeckii* (smaller leaves and red stems); *A. xanthochlora* (yellow-green leaves, very free-flowering).

PLANT PROFILE
HEIGHT 60cm (24in)
SPREAD 75cm (30in)
SITE Sun or partial shade
SOIL Average
HARDINESS Fully hardy
FLOWERING Early summer to early autumn

Alopecurus pratensis 'Aureovariegatus' Foxtail grass

A

WITH ITS BRIGHT YELLOW AND GREEN STRIPES, 'Aureovariegatus' can be grown individually in a border or in drifts in wild gardens. The new foliage has a vibrant effect when grown in full sun, and is followed by tall thin stems with small reddish-brown flowers that can be used in cut-flower displays, or left to stand over winter to add height and interest to the garden. To maintain the vigour of this grass when grown on heavy clay, clumps should be lifted and divided every few years, replanting only the younger outer sections. On poor soil, it may not grow to its full height.

OTHER VARIETY *A. pratensis* 'Aureus' (shorter grass, foliage with yellow margins and an inner green stripe)

PLANT PROFILE
HEIGHT To 1.2m (4ft)
SPREAD 40cm (16in)
SITE Sun or partial shade
SOIL Average
HARDINESS Fully hardy
FLOWERING Mid-spring to midsummer

A | *Alstroemeria ligtu* hybrids **Peruvian lily**

THESE SHOWY, ATTRACTIVE EXOTICS will self-seed to form colourful clumps – from white to pink, yellow, and orange – at the front of a border. The only thing they lack is scent. New types keep appearing in garden nurseries that flower over a long summer period. Provide them with a sunny place in the border, as well as free-draining soil as they dislike standing in cold, wet soil over the winter. Not being totally hardy, young plants should be covered with a thick mulch of compost in their first few winters.

OTHER VARIETIES *A. pygmaea* (smaller-growing, deep yellow flowers); *A. psittacina* (mauve-spotted stems, green flowers overlaid with red in summer).

PLANT PROFILE
HEIGHT 50cm (20in)
SPREAD 75cm (30in)
SITE Full sun
SOIL Free-draining
HARDINESS Frost hardy
FLOWERING Summer

Amicia zygomeris

THIS HIGHLY UNUSUAL, DESIRABLE PERENNIAL has exceptionally straight, hollow stems, like thin bamboos, which fire up to well over head height. The stems bear beautiful bright green leaves which from a distance look like large butterflies, their wings fully opened and flat. At the base of each leaf are small, flower-like growths with purple veins. Grown mainly for its foliage, the pea-like yellow flowers will appear only in mild areas. It should be grown on free-draining, rich soil – against a warm, sunny, sheltered wall is ideal – and will need a thick, protective winter mulch of compost. In cold areas, you can dig up the plant in the autumn, cut it back, and keep it potted up in a frost-free place indoors over winter.

PLANT PROFILE

HEIGHT 2.2m (7ft)

SPREAD 1.2m (4ft)

SITE Full sun

SOIL Fertile, free-draining

HARDINESS Frost hardy

FLOWERING Early and mid-autumn

A | *Amsonia orientalis* Blue star

THIS SLOW-GROWING PLANT, with its loose heads of small, violet-blue, star-shaped flowers, are ideal at the front of a bed or border. Sometimes known as blue star, amsonias are sun-loving and like free-draining soil, but they are by no means completely drought tolerant. Their compact clumps are very attractive when planted at the foot of shrub roses, hiding the base of their bare stems. Amsonias can be divided in the spring if more plants are required, and they are usually very reliable, rarely falling victim to pests or diseases.

OTHER VARIETIES *A. illustris* (taller-growing, light blue flowers); *A. tabernaemontana* (lance-shaped leaves, free flowering); *A. tabernaemontana* var. *salicifolia* (narrow leaves, flowerheads more open).

PLANT PROFILE
HEIGHT 50cm (20in)
SPREAD 30cm (12in)
SITE Full sun
SOIL Free-draining
HARDINESS Fully hardy
FLOWERING Early and midsummer

Anaphalis triplinervis Pearl everlasting

A

PLANT PROFILE

ATTRACTIVE WHITE FLOWERS are not the only reason for growing this plant – its grey-green, white-woolly leaves have even greater appeal. Like most silver-leaved plants it likes a hot site in the garden and good drainage, but if the soil dries out too much the stems will quickly start to wilt. It is also possible to grow it in slightly shaded, moist ground. Plant it either as part of a white colour scheme, or to offset contrasting rich blues and reds. The stems can also be cut and used fresh or dried for indoor flower displays, where they will look particularly effective within a green foliage arrangement.

OTHER VARIETIES *A. margaritacea* (smaller-growing); *A. triplinervis* 'Sommerschnee' (brilliant white bracts).

HEIGHT 80–90cm (32–36in)	
SPREAD 45–60cm (18–24in)	
SITE Full sun	
SOIL Free-draining	
HARDINESS Fully hardy	
FLOWERING Mid- and late summer	

Anchusa azurea 'Loddon Royalist'

THE EXCEPTIONAL, ROYAL BLUE FLOWERS of this plant are highly useful at the start of summer. Strong, erect stems hold up the flower spikes which look beautiful among aquilegias or with a yellow-stemmed bamboo behind. After the first flush of blooms, cut back the stems to encourage a second flowering. The key to success is free-draining, fertile soil – if the plant sits in wet winter soil it will quickly rot. Being short-lived, take root cuttings or replace every few years as young plants give a better show of flowers. The similar, though smaller, *Anchusa cespitosa* looks good in a rock garden.

OTHER VARIETIES *A. azurea* 'Feltham Pride' (compact, clear blue flowers); *A. azurea* 'Little John' (dwarf, long-lived, deep blue flowers).

PLANT PROFILE

HEIGHT 90cm (36in)

SPREAD 60cm (24in)

SITE Full sun

SOIL Fertile, free-draining

HARDINESS Fully hardy

FLOWERING Early summer

Anemone nemorosa 'Robinsoniana' Windflower

A

FOR PALE LAVENDER-BLUE FLOWERS, each with a creamy-grey back, 'Robinsoniana' is the form of windflower to choose. It likes rich, moist soil, but will tolerate drier conditions when dormant in the summer. Other good forms of the windflower include 'Flore Pleno' with its white double flowers, and 'Wilk's Giant' which has the largest flowers in this group. Grow windflowers in groups among bright yellow buttercups and pale yellow primroses for a highly effective spring carpet of colour.

OTHER VARIETIES *A. nemorosa* (vigorous, white, pink-flushed flowers); *A. nemorosa* 'Allenii' (deep lavender-blue flowers); *A. nemorosa* 'Bowles' Purple' (rich purple flowers).

PLANT PROFILE
HEIGHT 8–15cm (3–6in)
SPREAD 30cm (12in)
SITE Partial shade
SOIL Moist, fertile
HARDINESS Fully hardy
FLOWERING Spring to early summer

A

Anemone x *hybrida* 'Königin Charlotte' Japanese anemone

FOR BEAUTIFUL COLOURS, good height, and open, cheerful flowers, the Japanese anemone is indispensable for the late summer/autumn garden. 'Königin Charlotte' (also called 'Queen Charlotte') has large double pink flowers and, like most Japanese anemones, soon forms a big clump. It prefers rich, moist soil, but dislikes heavy wet ground over winter. Plant these tall perennials in borders, beside ornamental grasses, with late-flowering clematis and annual cosmos, and in front of *Hydrangea aspera* subsp. *sargentiana*. In long, dry summers water the roots well and then add a thick mulch of compost.

OTHER VARIETIES   *A.* x *hybrida* 'Elegans' (single, pale pink flowers); *A.* x *hybrida* 'Honorine Jobert' (white flowers with a yellow eye).

PLANT PROFILE
HEIGHT 1.2–1.5m (4–5ft)
SPREAD Indefinite
SITE Full sun or partial shade
SOIL Moist, fertile
HARDINESS Fully hardy
FLOWERING Late summer to mid-autumn

Anemonopsis macrophylla

A

FOR WILD OR WOODLAND AREAS, or any shady part of the garden, this is an excellent plant to choose. It has attractive, 8cm (3in) long leaves, and black wiry flower stems that shoot up through the foliage. From a distance, the small, scattered, cup-shaped, nodding flowers resemble hovering insects. The soil must be acidic, moist and on the rich side, and some protection from penetrating cold winds is important to prevent the foliage from suffering badly. A native of the mountainous woodland areas of Japan, it could also be used as a fringe plant for an ornamental Oriental-style garden.

PLANT PROFILE

HEIGHT 75cm (30in)

SPREAD 45cm (18in)

SITE Partial shade

SOIL Acid, moist, fertile

HARDINESS Fully hardy

FLOWERING Mid- and late summer

A | *Angelica gigas*

TALL, THIN, PURPLE-FLOWERING STEMS high above the dramatic large leaves inject colour to the edge of a wooded area or wild garden. A large plant that self-seeds prolifically in moist, fertile soil, it also suits a site close to a river bank or the edges of a natural pond, where its leafy growth provides cover and shade for frogs and toads. Although new shoots can be devoured by slugs and snails, they will not make much impact on a massed spread of plants. Angelica is a short-lived plant, but look out for self-sown seedlings near the parent and move them to a preferred position before they grow too large.

OTHER VARIETY *A. archangelica* (greenish-yellow flowers).

PLANT PROFILE

HEIGHT 1–2m (3–6ft)

SPREAD 1.2m (4ft)

SITE Full sun

SOIL Moist, fertile

HARDINESS Fully hardy

FLOWERING Late summer and early autumn

Anthemis tinctoria 'E.C. Buxton' Golden marguerite

A

PALE LEMON-YELLOW FLOWERS, with a slightly darker eye, add a bright and breezy note to the early summer garden and are an asset to cottage gardens and borders before the midsummer scheme comes into its own. The one problem is that plants are short-lived, although they can be easily propagated by dividing clumps in the spring or late summer; alternatively, early summer cuttings quickly take root. Deadheading should provide a second flush of flowers, though not quite as impressive as the first. There are many excellent alternatives for a big border.

OTHER VARIETIES *A. tinctoria* 'Kelwayi' (clear, mid-yellow flowers); *A. tinctoria* 'Sauce Hollandaise' (cream, almost white, flowers).

PLANT PROFILE	
HEIGHT 90cm (36in)	
SPREAD 90cm (36in)	
SITE Full sun	
SOIL Free-draining	
HARDINESS Fully hardy	
FLOWERING Summer	

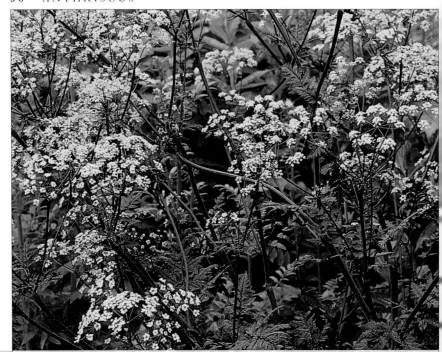

A

Anthriscus sylvestris 'Ravenswing' Cow parsley

THIS EASILY OVERLOOKED SHORT-LIVED PLANT has a superb open
structure of stems topped by white flowers above purple-brown
leaves. It is an essential component in a cottage or wild garden –
even in formal gardens, it adds a light and airy touch before the
main plants start performing. It can also be grown as a biennial, but
the easiest way to raise new plants is to look for seedlings scattered
around the parent and transplant them to a preferred position. Don't
cut off the flower heads too early or the seed will not have a chance
to ripen and scatter. Alternatively, you can collect the seed from the
flowers and sow it in the autumn in pots of seed compost. Keep the
seedlings outside in a sheltered position.

PLANT PROFILE
HEIGHT 1m (3ft)
SPREAD 30cm (12in)
SITE Sun or partial shade
SOIL Free-draining
HARDINESS Fully hardy
FLOWERING Mid-spring to early summer

Aquilegia vulgaris var. *stellata* 'Nora Barlow' Granny's bonnet

A

A QUINTESSENTIAL COTTAGE GARDEN PLANT, 'Nora Barlow' has downward-pointing pompons of pink and cream petals, unlike typical aquilegias with their open funnels. 'Nora Barlow' self-seeds freely around the garden and is happy in a wide range of situations and soils. The pastel flowers combine well with the royal blue *Anchusa azurea* 'Loddon Royalist', or grow it as part of a collection of aquilegias, which should also include the North American State and Songbird Series with their excellent colours and long spurs.

OTHER VARIETIES *A. caerulea* (blue and white flowers with slender spurs); *A. flabellata* (soft blue-purple flowers with white petal tips); *A.* Mckana Hybrids (vigorous, short-lived, in shades of blue, yellow, and red).

PLANT PROFILE
HEIGHT 90cm (36in)
SPREAD 45cm (18in)
SITE Full sun or partial shade
SOIL Moist, free-draining
HARDINESS Fully hardy
FLOWERING Late spring and early summer

A | *Arisaema candidissimum*

WONDERFULLY WEIRD AND SHAPELY, this is a deceptively easy plant to grow when given rich, neutral to slightly acid, moist soil and light shade among deciduous shrubs. *Arisaema candidissimum* sends up a quirky pink and white spathe (modified leaf), like a vertical funnel, with prominent lips and a protruding short point over the top which hides the real flowers deep inside it. Growth is not visible until early summer, and the leaf (there is only one) can grow up to 20cm (8in) long. Not totally hardy, it is best given a protective mulch of compost when the temperature dives during winter.

OTHER VARIETIES *A. amurense* (purple spathes with white stripes); *A. flavum* (small, yellow spathes); *A. tortuosum* (hooded green spathes).

PLANT PROFILE

HEIGHT 40cm (16in)

SPREAD 15cm (6in)

SITE Partial shade

SOIL Moist, fertile

HARDINESS Frost hardy

FLOWERING Summer

Arisarum proboscideum Mouse plant

A

THE DARK BROWN-PURPLE FLOWERS, which are actually modified leaves known as spathes, look like tiny animals with long whippy tails, and give rise to this plant's common name. These 'flowers' are tucked up among, and are often obscured by, the bases of the thin leaves, and in order to see them clearly it is important to place the mouse plant where it can be seen easily. Provide moist, rich soil and woodland-type conditions and it will spread to form large colonies. The tubers should be planted in autumn, at which time established clumps can also be divided. To do this, dig up a small patch, then carefully separate the tubers and replant healthy individual sections in similar growing conditions.

PLANT PROFILE

HEIGHT 15cm (6in)

SPREAD To 25cm (10in)

SITE Partial shade

SOIL Moist, fertile

HARDINESS Fully hardy

FLOWERING Spring

A | *Armeria maritima* 'Alba' Sea thrift

GROWING IN GRASSY LITTLE MOUNDS, this plant colonizes cliff tops and sea shores. The dark green, stiff, spiky leaves bristle on the ground and are topped by 20cm (8in) high flower stems, each with a rounded flowerhead. Sea thrift is easy to grow and likes poor to moderately fertile, free-draining soil – it will not be happy in moist or fertile conditions. It can be grown in rock gardens, as an edging plant or even in the top of a dry-stone wall. Divide established clumps in the spring and replant the outer sections.

OTHER VARIETIES *A. maritima* (profusely borne white, pink, or red-purple flowers); *A. maritima* 'Bloodstone' (dark red flowers); *A. maritima* 'Vindictive' (rose-pink flowers).

PLANT PROFILE

HEIGHT 20cm (8in)

SPREAD 30cm (12in)

SITE Full sun

SOIL Average, free-draining

HARDINESS Fully hardy

FLOWERING Late spring to summer

Artemisia ludoviciana 'Silver Queen' Western mugwort

A

THE SILVERY-WHITE LEAVES are the main feature of this plant rather than the plumes of brown-yellow flowers which some people remove before they open. 'Silver Queen' is at the top of any list for a white garden, and to keep it compact and encourage the attractive young leaves, prune it in spring. It can also be cut to the ground in the autumn and covered with a protective dry mulch during the winter. It does best in free-draining, fertile soil – in moist conditions it may not survive many years. *Artemisia absinthium* 'Lambrook Silver' is a superb alternative and also grows up to 75cm (30in) high.

OTHER VARIETIES   *A. glacialis* (lower-growing); *A. lactiflora* (creamy-white flowers); *A. schmidtiana* (small yellow flowers).

PLANT PROFILE
HEIGHT 75cm (30in)
SPREAD 60cm (24in)
SITE Full sun
SOIL Fertile, free-draining
HARDINESS Fully hardy
FLOWERING Midsummer to autumn

A

Arum italicum 'Marmoratum' Lords and ladies

WONDERFULLY PATTERNED, MARBLED LEAVES from winter to late spring, and a startling vertical yellow flower, make this a superb plant for a sheltered site. Even better, the flower is followed by bright orange-red berries that last until the end of summer. During its dormant summer period it likes to be on the dry side, after which new leaves start emerging in mid-autumn. Mulch with compost in winter and spring after heavy rain to keep moisture in the ground. Remove the mulch in summer. Note that the sap and juice of the berries can cause skin irritation, and the berries are toxic if ingested.

OTHER VARIETIES *A. creticum* (dark green, unmarked leaves); *A. pictum* (smaller-growing, blackish–purple spathes).

PLANT PROFILE

HEIGHT 30cm (12in)

SPREAD 15cm (6in)

SITE Sun or partial shade

SOIL Fertile, free-draining

HARDINESS Fully hardy

FLOWERING Early summer

Aruncus dioicus 'Kneiffi' Goat's beard

A

THIS IS A TALL, HIGH-IMPACT PLANT for the back of the border, featuring large sprays of tiny flowers held well clear of lacy, deeply divided leaves. Totally undemanding, it can be grown in most positions but thrives in shade and moist, rich soil – for example, by a stream or natural pond. 'Kneiffi' quickly self-seeds and spreads, but if you don't want any more plants you must cut off the flower heads as soon as they start to fade. The male creamy-white flowers and female greenish-white blooms are found on the same plant and make excellent cut flowers for flamboyant, architectural displays.

OTHER VARIETIES *A. aethusifolius* (shorter); *A. dioicus* (taller).

PLANT PROFILE
HEIGHT To 2m (6ft)
SPREAD 1.2m (4ft)
SITE Full or partial shade
SOIL Moist, fertile
HARDINESS Fully hardy
FLOWERING Early and midsummer

A

Arundo donax var. *versicolor*

SIMILAR TO A BAMBOO IN LOOKS and habit, this plant throws up impressive, stout stems with white-striped leaves that can grow up to 60cm (24in) long. Its green to purple flowers are unlikely to develop in northern Europe, even in good conditions and rich, moist soil, but this doesn't matter because it makes a superb foliage plant or summer screen, especially in a Japanese-style garden. Cut it back to the ground in the first half of winter to guarantee attractive fresh leaves the following spring. The parent of this variety, *Arundo donax* (giant reed), is the tallest hardy grass, growing up to 5m (15ft) high, and rarely needs staking.

OTHER VARIETY *A. donax* (mid-green leaves).

PLANT PROFILE

HEIGHT To 2m (6ft)

SPREAD 60cm (24in)

SITE Full sun

SOIL Moist, fertile

HARDINESS Fully hardy

FLOWERING Mid- and late autumn

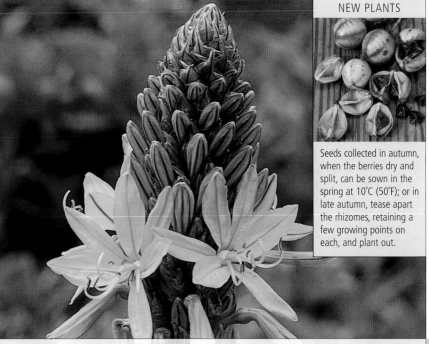

Seeds collected in autumn, when the berries dry and split, can be sown in the spring at 10°C (50°F); or in late autumn, tease apart the rhizomes, retaining a few growing points on each, and plant out.

Asphodeline lutea King's spear

A

EMERGING FROM LONG, SLENDER, BLUE-GREEN grassy foliage, these extraordinary plants send up erect spikes topped with open, star-like flowers. The straw-yellow, gently scented blooms are followed by impressive green berries. Grow it in a Mediterranean-style garden or at the base of a sunny wall in fertile, well-drained (but not arid) soil. If you want even more plants, they are easily propagated by seed, or by digging up the bulb-like rhizome and dividing it in late summer. Although fully hardy, in cold-climate gardens young plants will need a thick mulch of compost during their first couple of winters.

OTHER VARIETY *A. liburnica* (midsummer flowering).

PLANT PROFILE	
HEIGHT	1m (3ft)
SPREAD	30cm (12in)
SITE	Full sun
SOIL	Fertile, Free-draining
HARDINESS	Fully hardy
FLOWERING	Late spring

A

Asphodelus albus Asphodel

THIS COTTAGE GARDEN PLANT has erect stems, reaching 90cm (36in) high, covered with open white flowers right up to the top. Asphodel is a useful gap filler in the garden, requiring only free-draining soil and bright sun to look its best; if it is being grown in rich soil, however, it will grow even taller but will need staking to keep it erect. Grow it with tall alliums or an underplanting of red tulips for a dramatic effect. *Asphodelus fistulosus*, which has beautiful, small star-shaped flowers with a red line running up to the point of each petal, is a good alternative but more difficult to find.

PLANT PROFILE

HEIGHT 90cm (36in)

SPREAD 30cm (12in)

SITE Sun

SOIL Average, free-draining

HARDINESS Fully hardy

FLOWERING Mid- or late spring

Astelia chathamica

A

THIS PUNCHY, DRAMATIC EVERGREEN from New Zealand has sword-shaped, silvery-blue leaves that grow up to 1.2m (4ft) long. The yellowish-green flowers are insignificant. It needs moist, acid soil that should not be allowed to dry out, especially in summer when you must water it well during prolonged dry spells. In addition, water it in spring and then add a thick mulch of compost to help keep moisture in the ground through the growing season. Although it is not totally hardy, it will regrow in the spring if it is cut back by winter frost. Use it as a feature plant, where no other plants will compete with it and spoil the effect.

OTHER VARIETY *A. nervosa* (hardier, smaller-growing).

PLANT PROFILE
HEIGHT 1.2m (4ft)
SPREAD To 2m (6ft)
SITE Sun or partial shade
SOIL Acid, moist, fertile
HARDINESS Frost hardy
FLOWERING Mid- and late spring

Aster novae-angliae 'Purple Dome' New England aster

A

BLOOMING PROFUSELY right at the end of the season, injecting bright shades of pink, lilac, purple (*see inset*), and white, asters (commonly called Michaelmas daisies) are well worth their place in any border. Many grow up to 1.5m (5ft) high, but 'Purple Dome' is nicely compact. Divide it every three years to keep it vigorous, or take cuttings in spring. Like all New England asters, it prefers rich, moist soil and tolerates some shade. Unlike the true Michaelmas daisies, *Aster novi-belgii*, mildew is not a problem.

OTHER VARIETIES *A. novae-angliae* 'Andenken an Alma Pötschke' (salmon-pink flowers); *A. novae-angliae* 'Harrington's Pink' (light pink flowers); *A. novi-belgii* 'Kristina' large, (semi–double, white flowers).

PLANT PROFILE		
HEIGHT 60cm (24in)		
SPREAD 60cm (24in)		
SITE Sun or partial shade		
SOIL Moist, fertile		
HARDINESS Fully hardy		
FLOWERING Late summer to mid-autumn		

Aster pilosus var. *pringlei* 'Monte Cassino'

A

COVERED BY PROLIFIC SPRAYS of white daisy-like flowers, each with a yellow eye, this plant needs moist, rich soil to promote plenty of blooms, although it will not tolerate waterlogged conditions in the winter. If the ground is too wet, dig up the plant, keep it in a cool greenhouse and plant out the following spring. Alternatively, since 'Monte Cassino' flowers best in its first year, take cuttings in the spring and discard the parent after it has flowered. Plant the cuttings out 12 months later. The flower sprays make excellent cut flowers.

OTHER VARIETIES *A. alpinus* (smaller-growing, violet flowers); *A. amellus* 'Veilchenkönigin' (violet-purple flowers); 'Coombe Fishacre' (pink-flushed white flowers); *A. turbinellus* (pale violet flowers).

PLANT PROFILE
HEIGHT To 1m (3ft)
SPREAD 30cm (12in)
SITE Sun or partial shade
SOIL Moist but free-draining, fertile
HARDINESS Fully hardy
FLOWERING Late summer to mid-autumn

A

Astilbe x arendsii 'Fanal'

WITH ERECT, FLUFFY PLUMES of tiny, dark crimson flowers above the 23cm (9in) long leaves, 'Fanal' adds rich tones to a bog garden or very damp part of a border. Like all astilbes, it needs a permanently moist, fertile soil, with well-rotted compost added to it every year. Although flowering is restricted to early summer, the panicles gradually turn brown and continue into winter without looking ragged or tired. 'Fanal' makes an excellent backdrop to a wide range of moisture-loving plants from *Iris ensata* (Japanese flag) to *Ligularia*.

OTHER VARIETIES *A. x arendsii* 'Brautschleier' (white flowers); *A. x arendsii* 'Irrlicht' (white flowers, dark green leaves); *A. x crispa* 'Perkeo' (compact, deep pink flowers); 'Sprite' (shell-pink flowers).

PLANT PROFILE	
HEIGHT	60cm (24in)
SPREAD	45cm (18in)
SITE	Full sun
SOIL	Moist, fertile
HARDINESS	Fully hardy
FLOWERING	Early summer

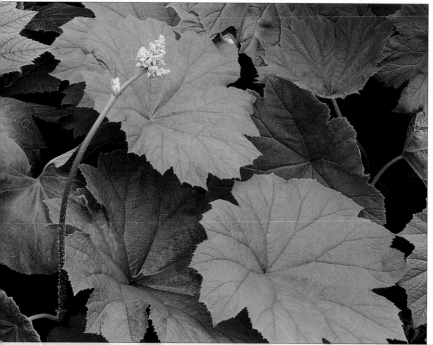

Astilboides tabularis

A

IF YOU WANT A WATERSIDE PLANT with big, bold foliage but don't have room for the very large and dominating *Gunnera manicata*, you can grow this Chinese perennial instead. Individual leaves are about 90cm (36in) long, and held on tall stems up to 1.2m (4ft) high, while the creamy-white flowers give the plant an extra 30cm (12in) of height in early and midsummer. The rounded leaves are lobed and toothed, making them even more dramatic, and they create the perfect shaded canopy for frogs to hide beneath. This plant needs to be grown in light shade on damp soil that never dries out.

PLANT PROFILE

HEIGHT 1.5m (5ft)

SPREAD 1.2m (4ft)

SITE Partial shade

SOIL Moist

HARDINESS Fully hardy

FLOWERING Early and midsummer

A

Astrantia major 'Hadspen Blood' Masterwort

THIS WONDERFUL VARIETY really stands out in a cottage garden. All types of masterwort have pincushion flowers on wiry stems and, as its name suggests, the blooms of 'Hadspen Blood' are dark red. It needs a sunny position to bring out its colours, unlike most other astrantias which thrive in shade. It also requires rich, moist soil to do well. Grow it with the white *Astrantia major* for contrast. Other red astrantias include 'Ruby Wedding' and 'Rubra', while *A. major* var. *rosea* has pink tints. Propagate 'Hadspen Blood' by division in spring; each section needs a growing point and its own root system.

OTHER VARIETIES *A. major* subsp. 'Shaggy' (long bracts with green tips); *A. major* 'Sunningdale Variegated' (leaves with creamy margins).

PLANT PROFILE
HEIGHT 90cm (36in)
SPREAD 45cm (18in)
SITE Full sun
SOIL Moist, fertile
HARDINESS Fully hardy
FLOWERING Early and midsummer

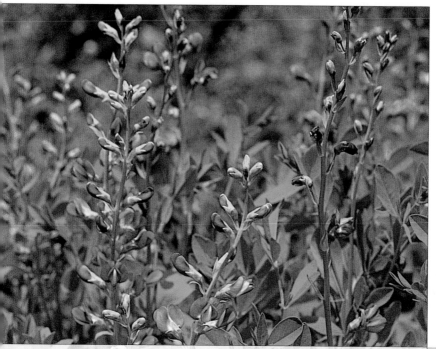

Baptisia australis Falso indigo

B

PRODUCING A GOOD SHOW of dark blue, pea–like flowers on erect stems held clear of the leaves, this plant really comes to life in early summer. Even when the flowers fade, the foliage gives a vigorous, fresh, bright look for the rest of the season. Its long roots need deep, rich, moist but well–drained soil, although it grows on sandy soil in the wild and will, therefore, also tolerate drier ground. Make sure you choose the right position from the outset because once in the ground, and well established, the deep roots dislike being disturbed.

PLANT PROFILE
HEIGHT 1.5m (5ft)
SPREAD 60cm (24in)
SITE Full sun
SOIL Fertile, moist but free-draining
HARDINESS Fully hardy
FLOWERING Early summer

B | *Belamcanda chinensis* Blackberry lily

AN INTRIGUING PLANT that needs to be the centre of attention in its own display, where it is not overshadowed by bolder, brasher plants. Its short, sword-like leaves grow straight out of the ground (like those of an iris), while the tall, slim stems carry star-like, yellow to orange-red flowers covered with maroon spots (*see inset*). There is a quick succession of flowers, each lasting only one day, and the blooms are followed by capsules containing large black seeds. Not totally hardy, you need to provide it with a thick winter mulch of compost or grow it in a sunny, sheltered site. Propagate by dividing plants in the spring, or by carefully forking young seedlings out of the ground and moving them to a prepared position in the garden.

PLANT PROFILE

HEIGHT 45–90cm (18–36in)

SPREAD 20cm (8in)

SITE Full sun or partial shade

SOIL Moist, fertile, free-draining

HARDINESS Frost hardy

FLOWERING Summer

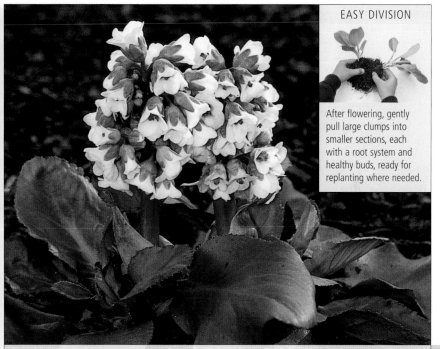

After flowering, gently pull large clumps into smaller sections, each with a root system and healthy buds, ready for replanting where needed.

Bergenia 'Bressingham White'

B

THIS FIRST-RATE, FRONT-OF-BORDER PLANT has large leaves with clear white flowers on short, strong stems. It makes a good backdrop to a pond where it should be planted in free-draining soil away from the water's edge, or to soften the straight edges of bordering paths. Other bergenias have leaves that redden up in the winter – the deep pink 'Eric Smith' being one of the best – and where plants are chosen for their leaf colour, an exposed site and poor soil is best; in other cases, plant in more fertile ground.

OTHER VARIETIES *B.* 'Ballawley' (bronze-purple winter foliage); *B. cordifolia* 'Purpurea' (magenta flowers, red leaves); *B.* 'Morgenröte' (reddish-pink flowers); *B. purpurascens* (beetroot-red winter foliage).

PLANT PROFILE	
HEIGHT 30–45cm (12–18in)	
SPREAD 45–60cm (18–24in)	
SITE Sun or partial shade	
SOIL Free-draining	
HARDINESS Fully hardy	
FLOWERING Mid- and late spring	

B | *Bouteloua gracilis* Blue grama

WHILE MOST GRASSES MAKE BIG CLUMPS, this is a gem of a short grass from the dry plains of southern North America. The brush-like, brownish-purple flowers stick out horizontally, and initially have a red hue before turning beige. Blue grama makes excellent fringe planting on the sunny side of an island bed, to the front of a border, and in gravel. It can be planted in geometric patterns – for example, in alternating squares – and can even be mowed where large clumps have formed. You need only buy a few plants because they self-seed quickly when grown in light, free-draining soil.

OTHER VARIETY *B. curtipendula* (taller, with smaller flowerheads).

PLANT PROFILE

HEIGHT To 50cm (20in)

SPREAD 30cm (12in)

SITE Full sun

SOIL Free-draining

HARDINESS Fully hardy

FLOWERING Summer

Boykinia aconitifolia

B

THIS MODEST, RELIABLE PERENNIAL is suitable for a half-shady site with moist, rich, acid soil. It produces sprays of white, bell-shaped flowers with a yellow-tinged centre, and attractive, rounded, deeply lobed leaves. Grow it in a wild or wooded area of the garden, or at the shady end of a border. Extra plants can be produced by dividing a clump in the spring and replanting the sections wherever they are needed in the garden.

OTHER VARIETY *Boykinia jamesii* (much shorter plant, with pinkish-red flowers)

PLANT PROFILE
HEIGHT 15–60cm (6–24in)
SPREAD 30cm (12in)
SITE Partial shade
SOIL Acid, moist, fertile
HARDINESS Fully hardy
FLOWERING Early and midsummer

B | *Briza media* Common quaking grass

THIS SHORT, LIGHT, AIRY GRASS makes a clump of fresh green leaves topped by stems with dangling, oat-like flowerheads. Initially the flowers are tinged red, but they gradually fade to beige. Quaking grass adds a fun touch when grown on the sunny side of fruit trees or in rock gardens, and is excellent for use in cut or dried flower displays. *Briza media* is easy to grow, and is adaptable to most soils, including light and heavy types. Large clumps can be divided in spring, and the old growth can be cut back in midsummer to promote fresh new leaves, although you will lose the attractive straw-coloured seedheads in the process.

OTHER VARIETY *B. maxima* (shorter, leaves edged with pale green).

PLANT PROFILE

HEIGHT 60–90cm (24–36in)

SPREAD 30cm (12in)

SITE Full sun

SOIL Moist

HARDINESS Fully hardy

FLOWERING Late spring to midsummer

Brunnera macrophylla

B

THIS FLOWERING GROUND-COVER PLANT has sprays of bright blue flowers, like forget-me-nots, among heart-shaped leaves. It is not so invasive that it ever becomes a major problem, and you can easily slice down through the roots with a spade and dig out any excess growth. It prefers light shade where the soil is moist, but if grown in a sunnier, more open position, mulch it well with compost after heavy rain to lock moisture in the ground. 'Hadspen Cream' has white markings on the leaf edges, as does the attractive 'Dawson's White'; both of these variegated varieties are best grown in shadier positions in the garden.

OTHER VARIETY *B. macrophylla* 'Betty Bowring' (white flowers).

PLANT PROFILE

HEIGHT 45cm (18in)

SPREAD 60cm (24in)

SITE Light shade

SOIL Moist

HARDINESS Fully hardy

FLOWERING Mid- and late spring

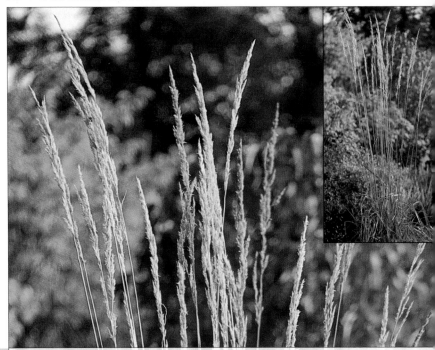

Calamagrostis x *acutiflora* 'Karl Foerster' Feather reed grass

THIS BEAUTIFUL GRASS FORMS A CLUMP of wonderful arching leaves from spring to winter. In summer, the ramrod-erect flowering stems that shoot up from the centre hold feathery red-tinged panicles that fade to beige and catch the breeze. Use 'Karl Foerster' in a gravel garden, or as a focal point in a border with low plants in front to allow it to be fully appreciated. It prefers free-draining fertile soil, but will still perform well in clay. Leave the flowering stems through winter to provide shape in the garden, but cut them back in early spring before the new growth appears.

OTHER VARIETY *C.* 'Overdam' (lower-growing, leaves with pale yellow margins and stripes).

PLANT PROFILE	
HEIGHT To 2m (6ft)	
SPREAD 60cm (24in)	
SITE Sun or partial shade	
SOIL Fertile, free-draining	
HARDINESS Fully hardy	
FLOWERING Mid- and late summer	

Calamintha nepeta Lesser calamint

C

A GOOD CHOICE FOR GRAVEL GARDENS, lesser calamint flowers in the second half of summer when many other garden plants lack colour. The mauve, sometimes pink, flowers attract butterflies and bees, and the leaves are scented. It grows wild in central France and the Pyrenees, and bright sun and free-draining soil are essential; it will not tolerate ground that stays cold and wet over winter. The dark pink *Calamintha grandiflora*, which grows to the same height, is slightly bushier and prefers light, dappled shade.

OTHER VARIETIES *C. grandiflora* 'Variegata' (aromatic, green and cream variegated leaves); *C. nepeta* subsp. *nepeta* 'White Cloud' (white flowers in spring and summer).

PLANT PROFILE	
HEIGHT To 45cm (18in)	
SPREAD 50–75cm (20–30in)	
SITE Sun or partial shade	
SOIL Free-draining	
HARDINESS Fully hardy	
FLOWERING Late summer	

C | *Caltha palustris* Kingcup

AN IDEAL PLANT FOR A BOG GARDEN or wet ground at the edge of a pond, where you can enjoy its flashy yellow blooms in the spring. The flowers are offset by the dark leaves and the brown, muddy ground. It is possible to grow kingcup in a border if you check that the soil is constantly wet. If you have the space for more than one plant, grow 'Flore Pleno', which has double yellow flowers. *Caltha palustris* var. *palustris* (giant marsh marigold) is the biggest and showiest of the kingcups, with flowers 8cm (3in) wide.

OTHER VARIETIES *C. palustris* var. *alba* (compact growing, white flowers); *C. leptosepala* (silvery-white flowers on leafless stems).

PLANT PROFILE

HEIGHT 10–40cm (4–16in)

SPREAD 45cm (18in)

SITE Full sun

SOIL Wet

HARDINESS Fully hardy

FLOWERING Spring

Campanula garganica 'Dickson's Gold' Adriatic bellflower

C

THIS TINY BEAUTY OF A CAMPANULA can be grown in pots, wall crevices or rock gardens. Although small, it is robust and thrives in moist but free-draining soil. Other good, short campanulas include the rich purple, self-seeding *Campanula poscharskyana* which is 15cm (6in) high, spreading to 50cm (20in), and the creamy-white *C. poscharskyana* 'E.H. Frost'. The deep purple *C. portenschlagiana* also reaches a height of 15cm (6in), and is similarly grown to soften path edges or to spread across the top and sides of a dry-stone wall.

OTHER VARIETIES (all short) *C. carpatica* (large, solitary, bell-shaped, blue, purple or white flowers); *C. carpatica* 'Weisse Clips' (abundant white flowers).

PLANT PROFILE

HEIGHT 5cm (2in)

SPREAD 30cm (12in)

SITE Sun or partial shade

SOIL Moist but free-draining

HARDINESS Fully hardy

FLOWERING Summer

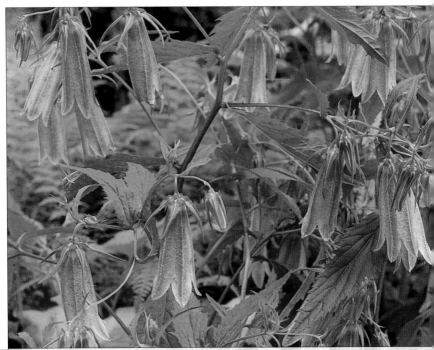

C

Campanula takesimana 'Elizabeth'

THE REDDISH–PURPLE TINGED FLOWERS with maroon speckling within are so attractive it's easy to ignore the plant's tendency to spread. If it does get out of hand, simply slice the roots with a spade and dig out the excess growth. The stems will need some support – twiggy sticks pushed into the soil as new growth appears in spring are ideal. Combine 'Elizabeth' with other medium-sized campanulas, such as *Campanula glomerata* (clustered bellflower), with its violet to lavender, or white flowers. Both need moist but free-draining soil.

OTHER VARIETIES (all medium) *C. alliariifolia* (tubular to bell-shaped white flowers); *C.* 'Burghaltii' (greyish lavender-blue flowers); *C. sarmatica* (hairy light grey-blue flowers).

PLANT PROFILE
HEIGHT 35–40cm (14–16in)
SPREAD 40cm (16in)
SITE Sun or partial shade
SOIL Moist but free-draining
HARDINESS Fully hardy
FLOWERING Summer

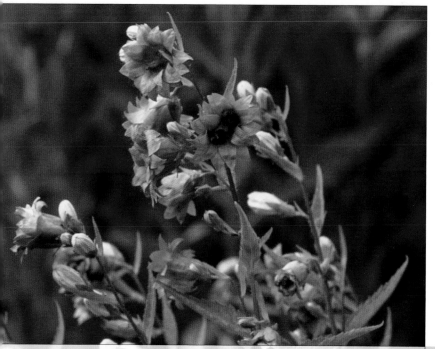

Campanula trachelium 'Bernice'

C

ALTHOUGH NOT THE VERY TALLEST CAMPANULA, 'Bernice' still needs staking to keep it upright. Its beautiful double lilac-blue flowers are perfect for the middle of a border in a cottage-style garden and it mixes well with the white 'Alba Flore Pleno', which also has double flowers. There are several other first-rate tall campanulas that will combine well with 'Bernice'. These include the white to pale blue *Campanula lactiflora* (milky bellflower), 1.2–1.5m (4–5ft) high and the lilac-pink *C. lactiflora* 'Loddon Anna'.

OTHER VARIETIES (all tall) *C. lactiflora* 'Alba' (pure white flowers); *C. latifolia* 'Brantwood' (deep violet flowers); *C. latiloba* 'Percy Piper' (rich lavender-blue flowers).

PLANT PROFILE		
HEIGHT 45–90cm (18–36in)		
SPREAD 30cm (12in)		
SITE Sun or partial shade		
SOIL Moist but free-draining		
HARDINESS Fully hardy		
FLOWERING Summer		

C | *Cardamine pratensis* 'Flore Pleno' Cuckoo flower

DOUBLE FLOWERS ON STIFF, ERECT STEMS, held well above the glossy dark green foliage, create a lilac-pink show in shady borders or wooded areas of the garden. Many of the cardamines are weeds, but the compact, clump-forming 'Flore Pleno' is well worth growing – as is 'Edith' which has double white flowers opening from pink buds. All cardamines like rich, moist soil, except for the smaller white-flowering *Cardamine trifolia* that prefers free-draining conditions.

OTHER VARIETIES *C. pentaphylla* (clump-forming with white, purple, or lilac flowers); *C. pratensis* (grey-green to glossy dark green leaves); *C. raphanifolia* (taller-growing).

PLANT PROFILE

HEIGHT 30–45cm (12–18in)

SPREAD 30cm (12in)

SITE Full or partial shade

SOIL Moist, fertile

HARDINESS Fully hardy

FLOWERING Late spring

Carex flagellifera Sedge

C

PLANT PROFILE

THE TALL, ARCHING THIN LEAVES of this New Zealand sedge make a small reddish-brown mound. In summer it sends up spikes with beige flowers followed by red-brown fruit. The bronze leaves look particularly effective when placed against vivid colours in a border or among tall perennials or shrubs with rich green foliage. Sedges are traditionally regarded as plants that require moist soil but there are many, such as *Carex flagellifera*, that thrive in drier ground.

HEIGHT 1.1m (3½ft)

SPREAD 90cm (36in)

SITE Sun or partial shade

SOIL Moist, free-draining

HARDINESS Fully hardy

FLOWERING Mid- and late summer

OTHER VARIETIES *C. berggrenii* (miniature, with tufts of blue-green leaves); *C. comans* (densely tufted, hair-like yellow-green, grey, or reddish-brown leaves); *C. morrowii* 'Fisher' (cream-striped leaves).

C | *Carex hachijoensis* 'Evergold' Sedge

THIS HIGHLY RATED SEDGE grows wild in Japan on dry, rocky slopes and in woods. Given similar garden conditions, particularly free-draining soil, it makes a beautiful mound of dark green leaves with pale yellow stripes. Its flowers are insignificant when compared with the foliage. Plant it in a gravel garden which provides the ideal free-draining soil conditions, while the stony surface sets off the foliage brilliantly. For a taller sedge that requires moist soil, try *Carex elata* 'Aurea' (Bowles' golden sedge), which is about twice the height of 'Evergold' and has arching yellow leaves margined with green.

OTHER VARIETIES *C. petriei* (pale pinkish-brown leaves); *C. pendula* (dense clumps of drooping green leaves).

PLANT PROFILE

HEIGHT 30cm (12in)

SPREAD 35cm (14in)

SITE Sun or partial shade

SOIL Free-draining

HARDINESS Fully hardy

FLOWERING Mid- and late spring

Catananche caerulea Cupid's dart

THIS CLUMP-FORMING PLANT has pretty, circular, open flowers that are usually lilac-blue, but can be darker or even white. It is a bright, breezy, cottage garden plant, ideal when a free-flowing display is required. It combines well with 'Bicolor' which is white with a purple eye. Grow Cupid's dart on free-draining soil in a bright, sunny position – when grown on heavier, wetter ground it soon deteriorates and dies. Cupid's dart also makes a good cut flower, brightening up any flower arrangement. Divide clumps every two years, and replant only the younger, fresher, more vigorous growth which will flower more freely.

OTHER VARIETY *C. caespitosa* (dwarf, yellow flowers in spring).

PLANT PROFILE

HEIGHT To 90cm (36in)

SPREAD 30cm (12in)

SITE Full sun

SOIL Free-draining

HARDINESS Fully hardy

FLOWERING Midsummer to autumn

C

Centaurea macrocephala Knapweed

THIS TALL-GROWING, BOLD PLANT needs a place at the back of the border. Its flowers, just like those of a thistle, are a rich, golden yellow, 5cm (2in) wide, opening on top of strong, stiff stems. The large leaves are rather coarse, but they add to the impact of the flowers. If space allows, there are other knapweeds (many are shorter) with purple, pink, blue, or white flowers. They all need free-draining soil and, while many are drought-tolerant, *Centaurea macrocephala* requires regular watering through the growing season or it will flop.

OTHER VARIETIES (all medium) *C. cineraria* (purple flowers, grey-white leaves); *C. dealbata* (white-centred pink flowers); *C. hypoleuca* 'John Coutts' (deep rose-pink flowers).

PLANT PROFILE

HEIGHT To 1.5m (5ft)

SPREAD 60cm (24in)

SITE Sun or partial shade

SOIL Moist but free-draining

HARDINESS Fully hardy

FLOWERING Midsummer

To support a floppy stemmed plant, use a ring of canes encircled with garden twine. Once the plant fills out, the support will be invisible.

Centaurea montana 'Alba' Mountain knapweed

C

THE VALUE OF THIS KNAPWEED is that it starts flowering in early summer, before the others, and has delicate, open, spider-like white blooms. It is slightly floppy and sprawling, however, and needs some support to keep it upright. To prevent the appearance of mildew, cut down plants the moment they have finished flowering, which eliminates the problem and promotes new growth. Other colours are available, including 'Carnea' (bright pink), 'Parham' (lavender-blue), and 'Violetta' (dark violet). Free-draining soil that stays moist in summer is essential for mountain knapweeds to flourish.

OTHER VARIETIES (all shorter) *C. bella* (feathery leaves, pink to purple flowers); *C. pulcherrima* (silvery-yellow bracts and pink flowers).

PLANT PROFILE

HEIGHT	45cm (18in)
SPREAD	60cm (24in)
SITE	Full sun
SOIL	Moist but free-draining
HARDINESS	Fully hardy
FLOWERING	Late spring to midsummer

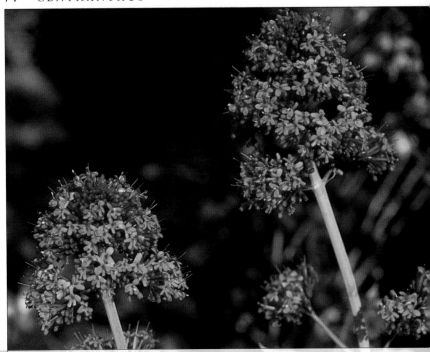

C | *Centranthus ruber* Red valerian

A MUST FOR COTTAGE GARDENS, this perennial produces a vigorous clump of crimson flowers on tall thin stems that stand well clear of the foliage. Given modest conditions – it prefers average soil with good drainage – it will produce a superb, free-flowering show throughout the summer. It also self-seeds freely, often in wonderful ways, popping out of stone walls, paving, gravel, and beds. It is a useful plant for making a lively, tasteful link between the formal and wilder, more natural parts of the garden. If you want to prevent it from self-seeding, cut back the flowers as soon as they fade. Pruning also promotes a second flush of blooms.

PLANT PROFILE

HEIGHT To 1m (3ft)

SPREAD To 1m (3ft)

SITE Full sun

SOIL Average, free-draining

HARDINESS Fully hardy

FLOWERING Spring to late summer

Cephalaria gigantea Giant scabious

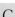

FOR A LIVELY, IMPRESSIVE DISPLAY, find room in the garden for a giant scabious. It produces a mass of long, thin, stiff-branched stems topped by small, pincushion flowers held high above the foliage. Find a gap at the back of a border or cottage garden where it can be seen clearly. It is best grown in rich, moist but well-drained soil, and the plant looks great contrasted with tomato-red crocosmias. It can also be used to the front of a statue or urn on a plinth, where the ornament will appear to rise up out of a tangle of stems and soft yellow flowers. New plants can be created for additional impact by dividing clumps in the spring or autumn.

OTHER VARIETY *C. alpina* (lower-growing, pale yellow flowers).

PLANT PROFILE
HEIGHT 2.5m (8ft)
SPREAD 60cm (24in)
SITE Sun or partial shade
SOIL Moist but free-draining, fertile
HARDINESS Fully hardy
FLOWERING Summer

C | *Ceratostigma plumbaginoides*

THE BRIGHT, RICH-COLOURED FLOWERS of this plant are a real bonus in a late-season garden, when the leaves also redden up to provide additional interest. This small plant's slim stems creep and crawl, nudging through adjoining plants. It is best appreciated when given a place right at the front of the border, in a rock garden, or planted in a dry-stone wall, where it will form a mat of growth. When grown in the border, it needs light, free-draining soil and a position sheltered from the effects of cold, wet winters. Young plants need extra protection in their first winter. They can either be potted up and brought into a conservatory or greenhouse, or left in the ground and covered with a thick blanket of bracken.

PLANT PROFILE

HEIGHT To 45cm (18in)

SPREAD 30cm (12in) or more

SITE Full sun

SOIL Free-draining

HARDINESS Fully hardy

FLOWERING Autumn

Chaerophyllum hirsutum 'Roseum'

C

LOOKING LIKE A PINK VERSION of *Anthriscus sylvestris* (cow parsley), *Chaerophyllum hirsutum* 'Roseum' has similar fern-like leaves and lovely sprays of flowers. It is traditionally grown in wild or cottage gardens, on the freer, outer edge of a formal garden, or backing an artificial pond. The white version is *C. hirsutum*, and both need to be grown in moist soil. If they self-seed, carefully dig up the seedlings in spring and transplant them where needed in the garden. Keep a lookout for slugs and snails, however, because these can devour the new shoots. This plant is sometimes called chervil, but don't confuse it with the herb (*Anthriscus cerefolium*).

PLANT PROFILE	
HEIGHT	60cm (24in)
SPREAD	30cm (12in)
SITE	Sun or partial shade
SOIL	Moist
HARDINESS	Fully hardy
FLOWERING	Late spring to midsummer

C | *Chamaemelum nobile* 'Flore Pleno' Camomile

TRADITIONALLY GROWN IN HERB GARDENS or as an edging plant at the front of a border, camomile spreads well without becoming invasive. 'Flore Pleno' has double white, yellow–eyed flowers, while *Chamaemelum nobile* produces single ones. The leaves of both emit a wonderful scent when crushed and are ideal for a lawn, where plants should be set 12–15cm (5–6in) apart, or a camomile seat. Water both freely until established, and keep trimming to encourage dense growth. Free-draining sandy soil is ideal, although camomile will tolerate most sites. The leaves can also be used to make tea, hair rinses and pot-pourris. Contact with the leaves can irritate the skin, however, and excessive ingestion can lead to vomiting.

OTHER VARIETY *C. nobile* 'Treneague' (strongly scented foliage).

PLANT PROFILE

HEIGHT 15cm (6in)

SPREAD 45cm (18in)

SITE Sun

SOIL Free-draining

HARDINESS Fully hardy

FLOWERING Summer

Chasmanthium latifolium Sea oats

THE COMMON NAME IS A BIT MISLEADING because sea oats is not specifically for coastal gardens. The foliage of this clump-forming American grass resembles that of a bamboo, and the plant will perform best when planted in moist, rich soil. The flower spikelets appear on slender stems right at the end of the summer or, more usually, in the autumn, and are initially green but then turn bronze and finally beige. They are worth leaving unpruned throughout winter in the hope that, if the weather is cold enough, they will be rimed by frost. This also allows the plant to self-seed. If you want to cut the spikelets back at the end of autumn, you can then use them indoors as part of a dried-flower arrangement.

PLANT PROFILE

HEIGHT 1m (3ft)

SPREAD 60cm (24in)

SITE Sun or partial shade

SOIL Moist, fertile

HARDINESS Fully hardy

FLOWERING Late summer and early autumn

C *Chelidonium majus* 'Flore Pleno' Greater celandine

THIS BRIGHT FLOWER can be grown at the edge of a woodland or on any spare patch of ground in the garden. It is remarkably unfussy and grows just about anywhere, but moist, rich soil in dappled light is ideal. It is said to start flowering when the swallows arrive and stop when they leave, and it certainly does bloom over a long period. It is short-lived but since it self-seeds freely, new plants keep appearing. 'Flore Pleno' has double yellow flowers; *Chelidonium majus* produces single ones.

PLANT PROFILE	
HEIGHT	60cm (24in)
SPREAD	20cm (8in)
SITE	Sun or light shade
SOIL	Moist, fertile
HARDINESS	Fully hardy
FLOWERING	Summer

Chelone obliqua Turtlehead

C

WITH SHOWY, DARK PINK OR PURPLE FLOWERS, said to resemble turtles' heads, this is a good choice for an autumn garden when the robust blooms can reliably withstand the worsening end-of-season weather. Their warm, rich colour makes them a big hit. The packed stems are stiff and erect, and rise up out of a thick mass of lower leaves. Turtlehead prefers rich, moist soil and will even grow in a bog garden, making it a real bonus for anyone with heavy clay soil. If there is any danger that the soil will become too dry, add a thick mulch of compost after the ground has been well watered.

OTHER VARIETY *C. glabra* (pink-tinged white flowers).

PLANT PROFILE

HEIGHT To 60cm (24in)

SPREAD 30cm (12in)

SITE Partial shade or sun

SOIL Moist, fertile

HARDINESS Fully hardy

FLOWERING Late summer to mid-autumn

C

Chionochloa conspicua Plumed tussock grass

THIS PLANT FORMS A TALL TUSSOCK OF STRAPPY, upstanding leaves with an attractive, reddish-brown tinge, although the high point is in the summer when the arching flower stems shoot up 2m (6ft). The flowers resemble those of an open, airy *Cortaderia* (pampas grass) and the stems make a good cut flower display. A warm, sheltered site is important because it is not totally hardy. Provide free-draining soil and grit around the neck of the plant to keep it relatively dry over the winter, and cover plants with a thick layer of bracken in cold areas as an added safeguard.

PLANT PROFILE

HEIGHT To 2m (6ft)

SPREAD 1m (3ft)

SITE Sun

SOIL Free-draining

HARDINESS Frost hardy

FLOWERING Mid- and late summer

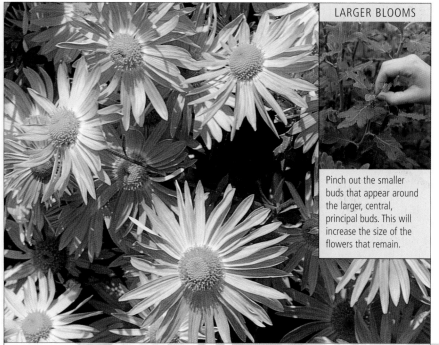

LARGER BLOOMS

Pinch out the smaller buds that appear around the larger, central, principal buds. This will increase the size of the flowers that remain.

Chrysanthemum 'Clara Curtis'

C

A PROFUSE MASS OF DAISY-LIKE, SCENTED FLOWERS with green eyes that gradually turn yellow makes this plant special. It is well worth its place in any border for its early autumn display, just when most plants are well past their best. Unlike many chrysanthemums, 'Clara Curtis' is fully hardy and needs no pampering in the greenhouse, although it is advisable to mulch over and around the plant with compost to provide extra winter protection. These chrysanthemums are easily propagated by cuttings taken in the spring.

OTHER VARIETIES C. 'Mary Stoker' (rose-tinted, apricot-yellow flowers); C. 'Nancy Perry'(semi-double, dark pink flowers).

PLANT PROFILE

HEIGHT 75cm (30in)

SPREAD 60cm (24in)

SITE Full sun

SOIL Fertile, free-draining

HARDINESS Fully hardy

FLOWERING Late summer to mid-autumn

C

Chrysogonum virginianum

EQUALLY GOOD IN THE BORDER or as a ground-cover plant at the wilder edge of a more formal garden, *Chrysogonum virginianum* has hairy, fresh green leaves and produces yellow, star-shaped flowers throughout the summer. It is not an aggressively invasive plant and can be controlled easily by slicing off the roots with a spade and digging out unwanted growth. It likes rich, moist but free-draining soil and combines well with *Vinca minor* 'Argenteovariegata' (lesser periwinkle) which has blue flowers and creamy variegated foliage. The periwinkle is also a vigorous plant and when combining these two, periodically cut back the *V. minor* to allow the yellow flowers of *C. virginianum* to show through.

PLANT PROFILE

HEIGHT 25cm (10in)

SPREAD 60cm (24in)

SITE Sun or partial shade

SOIL Fertile, moist but free-draining

HARDINESS Fully hardy

FLOWERING Early spring to late summer

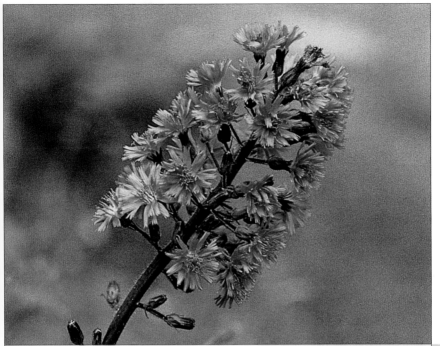

Cicerbita alpina Sow thistle

C

IMPRESSIVE TALL FLOWER SPIKES carry masses of blue, dandelion-like flowers well above head height, and make a colourful boundary to a wild garden. The sow thistle can also be grown at the back of a large border, although some people consider its appearance too coarse – especially the long leaves which can reach 25cm (10in) in length. It likes moist, rich, neutral to acid soil, and soon self-seeds to create a large display. In windy, exposed sites, the sow thistle may need staking to keep the spikes upright.

OTHER VARIETY *C. plumieri* (smaller-growing, clump-forming, blue flowers).

PLANT PROFILE
HEIGHT To 2.5m (8ft)
SPREAD 60cm (24in)
SITE Sun or partial shade
SOIL Moist, fertile
HARDINESS Fully hardy
FLOWERING Midsummer to early autumn

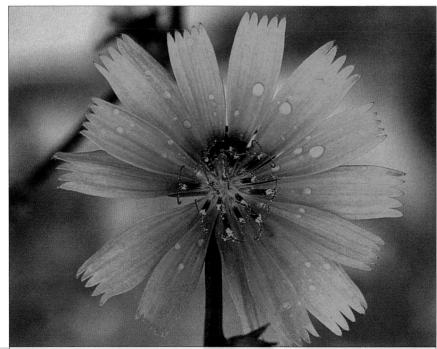

C | *Cichorium intybus* Chicory

GROWN WIDELY IN THE MEDITERRANEAN, chicory is suited to wild or herb gardens (the leaves can be used to make a mild laxative), or even kitchen gardens (the Romans grew it as a vegetable). It prefers full sun but will grow in some shade, and needs fertile, free-draining soil. The blue summer blooms, which can also be pink or white, look a little like dandelion flowers. Add the tender new leaves to salads, or boil them for a few minutes to reduce their bitter taste. The roots of a two-year-old plant can be sliced, roasted and used with, or instead of, coffee. Those with sensitive skin may find that the plant causes slight irritation.

OTHER VARIETY *C. spinosum* (dwarf with thistle-like blue flowers).

PLANT PROFILE	
HEIGHT 1.2m (4ft)	
SPREAD 60cm (24in)	
SITE Full sun	
SOIL Fertile, free-draining	
HARDINESS Fully hardy	
FLOWERING Summer	

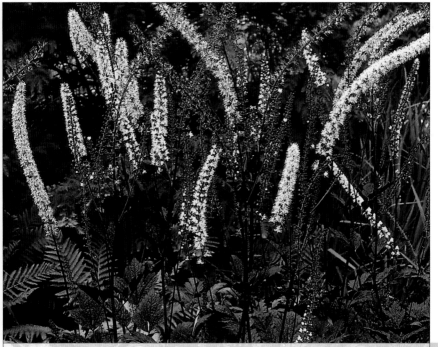

Cimicifuga simplex 'Brunette'

C

THIS IS A STRIKING BEAUTY with spires of purple-flushed flowers above dark bronze foliage. Look closely and you will see that the flowers have no petals, only stamens, but the effect is just the same. 'White Pearl' is a good close companion because of the contrast between its pure white flowers and the dark foliage of 'Brunette'. It prefers partial shade because the roots grow close to the surface and quickly dry out in hot sun. If grown in a sunnier site, water regularly and cover the soil with a thick mulch. The stems may need staking in windy gardens. Cimicifuga plants may also be sold as *Actaea*.

OTHER VARIETIES *C. japonica* (dark green leaves, pure white flowers); *C. racemosa* (dark green leaves, white flowers in midsummer).

PLANT PROFILE
HEIGHT 1–1.2m (3–4ft)
SPREAD 60cm (24in)
SITE Partial shade
SOIL Moist
HARDINESS Fully hardy
FLOWERING Early and mid-autumn

C   *Cirsium rivulare* 'Atropurpureum'

THIS EASILY GROWN, COLOURFUL THISTLE is just about the right size
for the majority of garden borders or wild gardens. The ground-
level, dark green leaves are 45cm (18in) long, and are more hairy
than prickly. The bare, vertical stems that shoot high above the leaves
are topped by richly coloured flowers, and the plant quickly forms
clumps, making an impressive show. Beware of experimenting with
other kinds of cirsium because many are very invasive, although the
rose-pink to lilac *Cirsium japonicum* is one that can be grown in
gardens. Both do well in moist but free-draining soil.

PLANT PROFILE
HEIGHT 1.2m (4ft)
SPREAD 60cm (24in)
SITE Full sun
SOIL Moist but free-draining
HARDINESS Fully hardy
FLOWERING Early and midsummer

Commelina coelestis Day flower

C

THE COMMON NAME OF THE DAY FLOWER comes from the fact that each bloom lasts only a day, but they form in such rapid succession that there is always a bright blue show. The plant's great virtue is the colourful flowers, which appear late in the season when other plants are fading. The day flower does tend to flop, though, and is typically used as ground cover. Plant it in a warm, sheltered site with free-draining soil, and because it's not reliably hardy, cover it with a thick, dry winter mulch or pot it up and keep it in the greenhouse over winter. Alternatively, use it as an annual filler for the border.

OTHER VARIETIES   *C. tuberosa* (green flowers streaked with dark blue-purple); *C. tuberosa* 'Alba' (white flowers).

PLANT PROFILE

HEIGHT To 90cm (36in)

SPREAD 45cm (18in)

SITE Sun or partial shade

SOIL Free-draining

HARDINESS Frost hardy

FLOWERING Late summer to mid-autumn

RHIZOME CUTTINGS

Rhizomes can be divided at any time of year, but after flowering is best. Cut them into about 8cm (3in) sections, each with roots and some dormant buds. Cover the sections in compost in a tray and plant out in the autumn once the roots are established and a new shoot is visible.

C | *Convallaria majalis* Lily-of-the-valley

THIS IS A TOP CHOICE for growing in the shade under trees where there is rich, moist soil. The erect pairs of leaves appear in the spring, followed by nodding, white, sweetly scented flowers. Don't hide it too far away in the shade because its beautiful small flowers need to be seen, and it's more vigorous when grown in dappled light. It spreads well but is never invasive, and excess growth can be dug out easily. When picking for cut flower displays, stand the stems in warm water for one to two hours.

OTHER VARIETIES   *C. majalis* 'Albostriata' (leaves striped creamy white); *C. majalis* 'Hardwick Hall' (leaves with narrow, pale green margins); *C. majalis* var. *rosea* (pale pink flowers).

PLANT PROFILE

HEIGHT 23cm (9in)

SPREAD 30cm (12in)

SITE Full or partial shade

SOIL Moist, fertile

HARDINESS Fully hardy

FLOWERING Late spring

Coreopsis verticillata 'Moonbeam' Tickseed

C

THERE IS AN ATTRACTIVE CONTRAST between the delicate, feathery foliage of this plant and its bright, lemon-yellow flowers. It stands up well at the front of a cottage garden or formal border, and provides opportunities for striking colour contrasts with reds and blues behind. Adjacent plants should flower in late summer to fill the gap left when the tickseed's blooms come to an end. It prefers free-draining soil but will tolerate heavier ground. 'Zagreb' has golden-yellow flowers, and 'Grandiflora' bears dark yellow blooms.

OTHER VARIETIES *C. grandiflora* (taller-growing, yellow flowers); *C. grandiflora* 'Early Sunrise' (semi-double, deep yellow flowers); *C. grandiflora* 'Mayfield Giant' (large, orange-yellow flowers).

PLANT PROFILE
HEIGHT 50cm (20in)
SPREAD 45cm (18in)
SITE Full sun or partial shade
SOIL Fertile, free-draining
HARDINESS Fully hardy
FLOWERING Early summer

C

Cortaderia selloana 'Pumila' **Pampas grass**

THIS STRIKING, STATELY, UPBEAT GRASS has silky plumes that make a real garden focal point. Being so large, it can be used only in sizeable borders, and is more often seen growing in a lawn (but beware of its sharp-edged leaves), or by a pond where it will reflect on the water. It likes free-draining but moist soil, and the crowns of young plants needs to be protected in their first winter with a thick mulch of bracken. Plumes can be left on all winter; prune them early in the spring before new growth emerges.

OTHER VARIETIES *C. richardii* (taller-growing, earlier-flowering); *C. selloana* 'Aureolineata' (yellow-margined leaves); *C. selloana* 'Rendatleri' (purple-pink heads); *C. selloana* 'Sunningdale Silver' (silver-white plumes).

PLANT PROFILE
HEIGHT 1.5m (5ft)
SPREAD 1.2m (4ft)
SITE Full sun
SOIL Moist but free-draining
HARDINESS Fully hardy
FLOWERING Late summer

Cortusa matthioli Alpine bells

C

SOMETIMES KNOWN AS ALPINE BELLS, this plant is a low-growing, colourful perennial that is suitable for a shady rock garden or under trees where the soil is moist and rich. Do not try growing *Cortusa matthioli* in a sunny border because it will not survive. The tiny magenta or purple-violet flowers dangle from slim stems and are held above crinkled, hairy leaves, similar to those of a primrose. Divide plants in the spring to increase your stock, and keep a lookout for possible slug and snail attacks.

OTHER VARIETIES *C. matthioli* 'Alba' (white flowers); *C. matthioli* subsp. *pekinensis* (magenta flowers).

PLANT PROFILE

HEIGHT 20–30cm (8–12in)

SPREAD 15cm (6in)

SITE Partial shade

SOIL Moist, fertile

HARDINESS Fully hardy

FLOWERING Late spring and early summer

C | *Corydalis flexuosa*

TO PROVIDE A COLOURFUL HIGHLIGHT in late spring, the brilliant electric-blue flowers of *Corydalis flexuosa* are perfect. It requires a shady spot, whether the sunless side of a dry-stone wall or shrub, or at the cool, moist end of a border, and is invaluable in cottage gardens because of its mix of leafy growth and small chirpy flowers. It mixes well with the bright yellow *C. lutea* which will also grow in full sun, and both need moist but free-draining soil. Other choices include 'Père David' (mid-blue) and 'China Blue' (pale blue).

OTHER VARIETIES   *C. cava* (purple or white flowers); *C. malkensis* (creamy-white flowers); *C. ochroleuca* (creamy-white flowers with a yellow throat); *C. solida* (mauve-pink to red-purple flowers).

PLANT PROFILE	
HEIGHT To 30cm (12in)	
SPREAD 20cm (8in)	
SITE Partial shade	
SOIL Moist but free-draining	
HARDINESS Fully hardy	
FLOWERING Late spring to summer	

Cosmos atrosanguineus

C

CHOCOLATE-SCENTED FLOWERS make this a novel plant for the garden. It is not a strong scent that wafts around – rather, you have to put your nose into its petals on a hot, sunny day – but it is fun to grow, and the dark maroon flowers are also an unusual colour. Grow it among whites, yellows and pastels to create a contrast. Not totally hardy, on cold wet clay it will probably die by midwinter. Ideally, plant it in a sunny, sheltered position in moist but well-drained soil, or pot it up in the autumn and keep it safe in a greenhouse until spring. Water the pots occasionally throughout the winter so that the soil does not dry out. If left outside all year, add a thick mulch of compost in winter which may help the plant to survive.

PLANT PROFILE
HEIGHT 75cm (30in)
SPREAD 45cm (18in)
SITE Full sun
SOIL Moist but free-draining
HARDINESS Frost hardy
FLOWERING Midsummer to autumn

C | *Crambe cordifolia*

THIS MAGNIFICENT PLANT throws out strong, angled, open stems that hold sprays of small, sweetly scented white flowers high above the leaves. Ensure you provide it with plenty of space in the border, where it will create an eye-catching, billowing aerial show of starry blooms. After the display, in the second half of summer, the dark green shiny leaves, which can reach 35cm (14in) wide, become the dominant feature. Free-draining, average soil is the key requirement to success, which is why you often see it thriving in coastal gardens, but it will need some protection in exposed, windy sites.

OTHER VARIETY *C. maritima* (blue-green leaves and profusely borne white flowers).

PLANT PROFILE
HEIGHT 2.5m (8ft)
SPREAD 1.5m (5ft)
SITE Full sun or partial shade
SOIL Average, free-draining
HARDINESS Fully hardy
FLOWERING Late spring and midsummer

Crepis incana Pink dandelion

C

ORIGINATING IN GREECE, where it grows in rocky, mountainous sites, the pink dandelion should be highly valued and ought to be far more popular. The flowers are a rich pink, and the rosettes of hairy leaves are grey-green with jagged edges. The flowers are at their best during the second half of the summer, and add a novel touch to rock or gravel gardens, where the plants will self-seed when the blooms are left unpruned. Bright sun and excellent drainage are essential because if the roots sit in damp soil over winter they will quickly rot.

OTHER VARIETY *C. aurea* (golden-orange flowers).

PLANT PROFILE	
HEIGHT	To 30cm (12in)
SPREAD	To 30cm (12in)
SITE	Full sun
SOIL	Free-draining
HARDINESS	Fully hardy
FLOWERING	Late summer

C

Crocosmia 'Lucifer'

THIS ELECTRIFYINGLY BRIGHT, brief-flowering plant with tomato-red flowers has great shock value. The small flowers are borne toward the tips of arching stems and hover in the air, well clear of the ground. The sword-like leaves are bright, fresh green. Place it close to evergreen shrubs that are not in flower to give them a lift, or use it to arch out over ponds, but plant in free-draining soil away from the moist ground by the water's edge. Divide clumps in spring.

OTHER VARIETIES *C.* x *crocosmiiflora* 'Emily McKenzie' (downward-facing, bright orange flowers with maroon markings); *C.* x *crocosmiiflora* 'Jackanapes' (bicoloured orange-red and yellow flowers); *C.* x *crocosmiiflora* 'Lady Hamilton' (golden-yellow flowers).

PLANT PROFILE
HEIGHT 1.1m (3½ft)
SPREAD 8cm (3in)
SITE Full sun or dappled shade
SOIL Fertile, free-draining
HARDINESS Frost hardy
FLOWERING Mid- to late summer

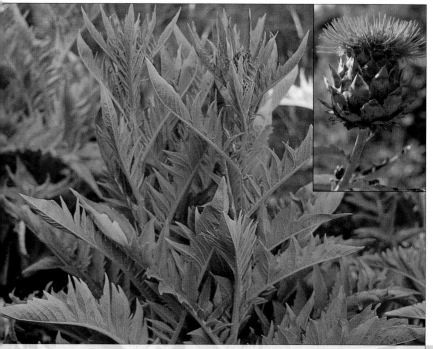

Cynara cardunculus Cardoon

C

THIS IS THE ULTIMATE THISTLE. A superb perennial, it spires straight up, firing out huge, horizontal, silver-grey leaves, nearly 60cm (24in) long and 35cm (14in) wide. The rich purple flowers are held on top of strong straight stems. Place it at the back of a wide border but make sure the plants in front don't obscure it. Alternatively, grow it as a feature plant in a wild part of the garden. Leave the stems over winter as an architectural, skeletal shape, but cut them down before the new growth starts in spring. It grows well in free-draining soil, which you should enrich each spring by forking in well-rotted manure around the root area, but not close to the crown.

OTHER VARIETY *C. scolymus* (edible flower buds, purple flowers).

PLANT PROFILE	
HEIGHT 1.5m (5ft)	
SPREAD 1.2m (4ft)	
SITE Full sun	
SOIL Free-draining	
HARDINESS Fully hardy	
FLOWERING Early summer to early autumn	

C

Cynoglossum nervosum Hound's tongue

THIS IS JUST ABOUT THE ONLY perennial hound's tongue grown in gardens. Similar to the forget-me-not (*Myosotis*), it features sprays of small blue flowers above bristly stems and hairy leaves. It is perfectly happy on average, even poor ground (avoid heavy clay and very fertile conditions), but will do best in moist but free-draining soil. The blue flowers mix well with the white flowers of snow-in-summer (*Cerastium tomentosum*), but make sure it does not become swamped by this vigorous, spreading plant.

OTHER VARIETY *C. amabile* (taller-growing, blue flowers, occasionally pink or white).

PLANT PROFILE

HEIGHT 60cm (24in)

SPREAD 60cm (24in)

SITE Sun or partial shade

SOIL Average, moist but free-draining

HARDINESS Fully hardy

FLOWERING Mid-spring to midsummer

Dactylis glomerata 'Variegata'

D

IN THE WILD THIS GRASS is used for grazing, and it can often be seen growing by the side of roads. In the garden, however, it needs some pampering to keep it looking smart. Groom out the dead leaves in the spring and autumn (use your splayed, open fingers to comb them out), and the brightly variegated foliage will give you a good show in return. *Dactylis glomerata* 'Variegata' forms a dense tuft, and the pale green flower spikes appear throughout the summer. The stems can be left standing over the winter months and cut back the following spring before the new shoots emerge.

PLANT PROFILE

HEIGHT To 45cm (18in)

SPREAD 25cm (10in)

SITE Sun or partial shade

SOIL Fertile, free-draining

HARDINESS Fully hardy

FLOWERING Summer

Store tubers over winter in a cool, frost-free place. When the leaves are blackened by frost cut the stems down, ease the tubers out of the ground, and remove excess soil. Place the tubers upside down for about 3 weeks in a box. Once dry, dust with fungicide and place the stems, right way up, in bark chips. Keep them dry until ready to plant out again in late spring.

D

Dahlia 'Bishop of Llandaff'

SOME OF THE MOST EXCITING FLOWER COLOURS are provided by dahlias. They come in rich reds and purples, yellows and oranges, as well as paler shades, with flowers in all shapes and sizes. 'Bishop of Llandaff' has bright red flowers, set against dark, almost black, shiny leaves. It is perfect for a fiery summer border or a gravel garden where its beautiful foliage contrasts well with the light stones. Plant out the tubers in free-draining soil in spring when there is no further danger of a hard frost

OTHER VARIETIES *D.* 'Chimborazo' (dark maroon flowers with yellow centres); *D.* 'Davenport Sunlight' (vivid yellow flowers); *D.* 'Hamari Bride' (pure white flowers); *D.* 'Wootton Cupid' (sugar-pink flowers).

PLANT PROFILE

HEIGHT 1.1m (3½ft)

SPREAD 45cm (18in)

SITE Full sun

SOIL Fertile, free-draining

HARDINESS Half hardy

FLOWERING Midsummer to late autumn

Darmera peltata Umbrella plant

D

SOMETIMES CALLED THE UMBRELLA PLANT, this slowly spreading perennial forms a striking umbrella-like clump of dark green leaves up to 45cm (18in) wide, which turn a wonderful ruby red in the autumn. The leaves are preceded in spring by the flowers which make flat heads of pale pink. It is suitable for planting in a pond or by the edge of a stream where its creeping roots will help to bind the muddy soil and prevent it from being eroded by the moving water. Established clumps can be divided in the spring, but don't be tempted to replant them near a small pond because they will soon outgrow their welcome and swamp the water feature.

PLANT PROFILE

HEIGHT	To 2m (6ft)
SPREAD	1m (3ft)
SITE	Sun or partial shade
SOIL	Wet
HARDINESS	Fully hardy
FLOWERING	Late spring

D | *Delphinium* 'Black Knight' Delphinium

DELPHINIUMS ARE A FANTASTIC SIGHT in the garden where they make clumps of tall, upright spires clothed in cup-shaped flowers. 'Black Knight' is a striking, dark purple example, perfect for the back of a cottage garden-style border, where it can be mixed with contrasting pink, white and red flowers. Stake plants in exposed, windy sites and protect them from slugs, especially in spring as the young growth emerges. There are dozens of other blues to choose from, including the mid-blue 'Blue Nile' and pale blue 'Skyline'.

OTHER VARIETIES *D.* 'Blue Dawn' (pale blue flowers); *D.* Belladonna Group 'Casa Blanca' (white flowers); *D.* 'Emily Hawkins' (violet flowers); *D.* 'Rosemary Brock' (deep pink flowers); *D.* 'Tiddles' (mauve flowers).

PLANT PROFILE

HEIGHT 1.2–1.5m (4–5ft)

SPREAD 60cm (24in)

SITE Full sun

SOIL Fertile, free-draining

HARDINESS Fully hardy

FLOWERING Early to midsummer

Deschampsia cespitosa 'Goldschleier' Tufted hair grass

D

THIS EXCELLENT GRASS has long, thin, strappy green leaves, and in summer produces dozens of erect stems with tiny, silver-tinged purple flowers which turn silvery and then beige. Leave the stems through winter to add extra shape to the garden, but cut them off the following spring before the new growth emerges. The silvery flowers stand out best against a dark background, such as a thick beech hedge. Tufted hair grass is happy in most soils, including clay that has had lots of compost added to it, to improve the drainage.

OTHER VARIETIES *D. cespitosa* (taller-growing); *D. cespitosa* 'Goldtau' (compact, with silver reddish-brown flowers); *D. flexuosa* 'Tatra Gold' (yellow-green leaves, bronze-tinted flowers).

PLANT PROFILE
HEIGHT To 1.2m (4ft)
SPREAD To 1.2m (4ft)
SITE Sun or partial shade
SOIL Free-draining
HARDINESS Fully hardy
FLOWERING Early to late summer

D | *Dianthus* 'Doris' Carnation

AVAILABLE IN A WIDE COLOUR RANGE, from white ('Hatyor White') to flashy red and yellow ('Bookham Fancy'), carnations, or pinks, are quintessential cottage garden plants. Many emit a sweet scent of cloves – the old-fashioned types, such as the white 'Mrs Sinkins', have the best scent, although many modern hybrids, such as 'Doris', are also perfumed. All need free-draining soil; without it, grow them in a raised bed, rock garden or tub. Deadheading encourages a long succession of flowers throughout the summer.

OTHER VARIETIES *D.* 'Dad's Favourite' (semi-double, white flowers); *D.* 'Inchmery' (double, lavender-pink flowers); *D.* 'Monica Wyatt' (double, pale lavender-pink flowers with magenta centres.).

PLANT PROFILE

HEIGHT 25–45cm (10–18in)

SPREAD 40cm (16in)

SITE Full sun

SOIL Free-draining

HARDINESS Fully hardy

FLOWERING Summer

Diascia 'Blackthorn Apricot'

D

MAKING A CLUMP OF VERTICAL SPIKES of pastel-coloured flowers, this is one of the best perennials for non-stop summer flowering and is great for the front of a border. Cut it back in midsummer to prevent it becoming straggly and to encourage even more blooms. Not totally hardy, it needs a sheltered, free-draining site, or dig up a clump in autumn for potting up and overwintering in the greenhouse. Alternatively, take cuttings in early summer to produce new plants. While free-draining soil is important, diascias need a regular water supply throughout the summer.

OTHER VARIETIES *D. integerrima* (purplish-pink flowers); *D. barberae* 'Ruby Field' (rich salmon-pink flowers).

PLANT PROFILE		
HEIGHT 25cm (10in)		
SPREAD To 50cm (20in)		
SITE Full sun		
SOIL Free-draining		
HARDINESS Frost hardy		
FLOWERING Summer to autumn		

D   *Dicentra* 'Langtrees'

THIS DAPPLED SHADE– AND DAMP-LOVING PLANT is good value, and
particularly suitable for cottage gardens and formal borders. Some
varieties of dicentra shoot everywhere but 'Langtrees' is a short,
compact, non-invasive spreader with pink-tinged flowers. It can
be grown close to *Dicentra spectabilis* (bleeding heart) where its tall
arching stems of pink, dangling flowers will create a light canopy
above 'Langtrees'. Both dicentras make successful ground cover
in gardens where the soil never dries out.

OTHER VARIETIES *D.* 'Adrian Bloom' (rich red flowers);
D. 'Bacchanal' (crimson flowers); *D.* 'Bountiful' (purple-pink flowers;
D. 'Luxuriant' (red flowers); *D.* 'Stuart Boothman' (deep pink flowers).

PLANT PROFILE

HEIGHT 30cm (12in)

SPREAD 45cm (18in)

SITE Partial shade

SOIL Moist

HARDINESS Fully hardy

FLOWERING Mid-spring to
midsummer

Dictamnus albus var. *purpureus* Burning bush

D

THIS IS A TRUE PARTY-PIECE of a perennial. On warm, summer evenings it releases tiny amounts of volatile oil – to see how its common name came about, simply light a match at the base and intermittent spurts of flame are produced. It looks a little like the flicker of flame produced if you ignite a dribble of alcohol on a Christmas pudding. Even if the trick does not work, it is still a choice garden plant. Tall and stately, it has leathery leaves smelling of lemons when crushed, and spikes of purple-mauve flowers, followed by seed pods that erupt and catapult seed all around when ripe. Give it rich, fertile, free-draining soil and select the right position first time because it dislikes being moved once it's established.

PLANT PROFILE

HEIGHT 40–90cm (16–36in)

SPREAD 60cm (24in)

SITE Full sun or partial shade

SOIL Fertile, free-draining

HARDINESS Fully hardy

FLOWERING Early summer

D

Dierama pulcherrimum Angel's fishing rod

THIS STAR PLANT HAS ARCHING, graceful flower stems that ascend out of a central evergreen clump of foliage. The dangling bell-shaped flowers are about 5cm (2in) long and sway in the wind, bringing colour and movement to the garden. Plant it toward the front of a border where it can arch over a wide path, or site it by a pond to overhang the water. It needs moist, rich soil and a sheltered position because it is not totally hardy, and remember that young plants may take a few years to flower. When it is well established, you can divide clumps in the spring.

OTHER VARIETIES *D. pulcherrimum* 'Blackbird' (rich purple flowers); *D. pendulum* (purple-pink flowers); *D. dracomontanum* (pink to red flowers).

PLANT PROFILE

HEIGHT 1–1.5m (3–5ft)

SPREAD 60cm (24in)

SITE Full sun

SOIL Moist, fertile

HARDINESS Frost hardy

FLOWERING Summer

Digitalis x *mertonensis* Foxglove

D

MOST FOXGLOVES ARE BIENNIALS (growing, flowering, and dying in two years), but this is a short-lived perennial, with spires of large, open-mouthed, strawberry-pink flowers that are loved by bees. The dark green leaves make a good contrast. It will flourish when grown on the shady side of the garden, or close to a woodland setting. Any seedlings can be carefully forked out of the ground and transplanted to other parts of the garden, or you can collect seed in the autumn and sow it in pots. Keep in a cold frame over the winter.

OTHER VARIETIES *D. davisiana* (pale yellow flowers); *D. ferruginea* (golden-brown flowers veined with red-brown); *D. grandiflora* (pale yellow flowers); *D. parviflora* (dark orange-brown flowers).

PLANT PROFILE
HEIGHT To 90cm (36in)
SPREAD 30cm (12in)
SITE Partial shade
SOIL Moist, fertile
HARDINESS Fully hardy
FLOWERING Late spring and early sumer

D | *Disporopsis pernyi* Fairy bells

THIS REMARKABLY EASY-TO-GROW PERENNIAL does best if provided with moist but well-drained soil in either a shady part of the garden or on the shady side of an evergreen shrub. It has decorative mottled stems and produces shiny, dark green leaves that remain evergreen, unless caught in freezing temperatures. The lemon-scented flowers are flared at the tips, and appear in late spring or early summer. You can easily obtain more plants by dividing the bulb-like underground growths in the spring, but make sure that each division has at least one good shoot and its own roots.

PLANT PROFILE

HEIGHT 40cm (16in)

SPREAD 30–40cm (12–16in)

SITE Partial shade

SOIL Moist but free-draining

HARDINESS Fully hardy

FLOWERING Early summer

Dodecatheon meadia f. *album* Shooting stars

D

THE SWEPT-BACK PETALS of the dodecatheons account for their common name. This eye-catching plant produces a clump of leaves, about 20cm (8in) long, which burst out of the ground with the strong, thin, flowering stems. Grow it in a shady rock garden or area under trees where its delicate flowers combine well with bluebells which enjoy the same rich, moist but well-drained soil conditions. Beware of slugs and snails, which can ruin the display.

OTHER VARIETIES *D. clevelandii* (reddish-purple flowers); *D. hendersonii* (crimson-pink flowers); *D. dentatum* (shorter with white flowers); *D. pulchellum* (deep cerise-pink flowers with dark centres).

PLANT PROFILE
HEIGHT 40cm (16in)
SPREAD 25cm (10in)
SITE Partial shade
SOIL Moist but free-draining, fertile
HARDINESS Fully hardy
FLOWERING Mid- and late spring

D | *Doronicum orientale* 'Magnificum' Leopard's bane

THESE QUINTESSENTIAL SPRING PLANTS produce large, daisy-like, bright yellow blooms, held well clear of the foliage. Leopard's bane is extremely easy to grow in most gardens, especially in the middle of a border or wild area, and likes moist but free-draining soil. It also makes a lively backdrop to a wide assortment of spring bulbs. Plant 'Magnificum' close to neighbours that offer eye-catching flowers in mid- to late summer because it tends to die down at this time. Other forms of *Doronicum orientale* offer lemon-yellow flowers ('Gerhard') and double flowers ('Frühlingspracht').

OTHER VARIETIES *D. columnae* 'Miss Mason' (large, bright yellow flowers); *D. x excelsum* 'Harpur Crewe' (larger-growing).

PLANT PROFILE
HEIGHT 50cm (20in)
SPREAD 90cm (36in)
SITE Partial shade
SOIL Moist but free-draining
HARDINESS Fully hardy
FLOWERING Mid- and late spring

Dracunculus vulgaris

D

THERE ARE THREE GOOD REASONS for growing this perennial. First, the mottled shoots that emerge from the ground look snake-like; second, the astonishing flowers, which last a week and immediately catch the eye; and, third, the incredibly disgusting scent is like that of a putrid drain and is often a big hit with children. The rotten smell is designed to attract pollinating insects in the Mediterranean countries where it grows naturally. Although it is not totally hardy, it will survive in cooler climates in well-drained soil that becomes quite dry in summer, and when given a protective winter mulch of compost. For plants with similar flowers, but without the smell, try arums.

PLANT PROFILE

HEIGHT To 1.5m (5ft)

SPREAD 60cm (24in)

SITE Full sun

SOIL Fertile, free-draining

HARDINESS Frost hardy

FLOWERING Spring or summer

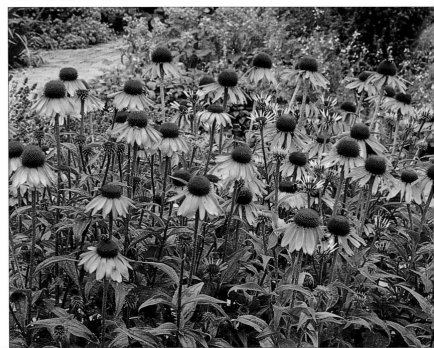

E — *Echinacea purpurea* Coneflower

NEITHER SUBTLE NOR SHY, this plant has large pink flowers with central, orange-golden-brown cones that are loved by bees and butterflies. Standing upright without staking, the coneflower adds colour and substance to borders in cottage or gravel gardens in the second half of summer. It thrives in fertile, well-drained soil and sun, and stocks can be increased easily by dividing plants in the spring or autumn. Other useful colours to combine with this one include white, pinkish-crimson and dark orange.

OTHER VARIETIES *E. purpurea* 'Magnus' (extra large, dark-orange flowers); *E. purpurea* 'White Lustre' (creamy-white flowers).

PLANT PROFILE

HEIGHT	1.5m (5ft)
SPREAD	45cm (18in)
SITE	Full sun
SOIL	Fertile, free-draining
HARDINESS	Fully hardy
FLOWERING	Midsummer to early autumn

Once the seedheads are dry and have turned brown, cut off the stems and pick off the seeds. Place them in a paper bag to dry and store until you are ready to sow them in a seedbed in the spring.

E

Echinops bannaticus 'Taplow Blue' Globe thistle

SPHERICAL, BRIGHT BLUE FLOWERS, about 5cm (2in) wide, on top of sturdy, thin stems provide an extra dimension to the middle or back of a border. The flowers are held high above jagged, spiny, hairy, grey-green leaves, and the plants soon form decent clumps when grown on dry, free-draining soil. Globe thistles are susceptible to mildew and if badly affected may need to be sprayed in late summer with a fungicide. Other choices include 'Blue Globe' with dark blue flowers, and the shorter *Echinops ritro* with bright blue globes.

OTHER VARIETIES *E. bannaticus* (blue-grey flowers); *E. ritro* 'Veitch's Blue' (smaller-growing, dark blue flowers); *E. sphaerocephalus* (vigorous, grey flowers).

PLANT PROFILE	
HEIGHT 1.5m (5ft)	
SPREAD 60cm (24in)	
SITE Full sun	
SOIL Free-draining	
HARDINESS Fully hardy	
FLOWERING Mid- and late summer	

E

Echium pininana

ALTHOUGH IT TAKES THREE YEARS TO FLOWER and then immediately dies, it is well worth the wait just to see the Canary Island *Echium pininana* in its full glory. It forms a rosette of dark green, hairy leaves about 7cm (3in) long, out of which shoots an astonishing stem, 1.5-4m (5-12ft) high, covered with bluey-mauve flowers. A mild climate without hard frosts is essential for it to survive the winter, and it likes free-draining, reasonably fertile soil. Given these conditions, it will self-seed after flowering. This amazing plant fits into the category of 'astonishingly exotic', and probably 'extremely odd' to anyone who prefers traditional borders, but it is a must for lovers of striking, architectural plants.

PLANT PROFILE

HEIGHT To 4m (12ft)

SPREAD 90cm (36in)

SITE Full sun

SOIL Fertile, free-draining

HARDINESS Frost hardy

FLOWERING Mid- and late summer

Elymus magellanicus Wild rye

E

WITH ITS ASTONISHING, INTENSE BLUE LEAVES, this is a grass with
real panache. Scattering gravel around the plant highlights its colour.
It needs excellent drainage – slopes provide an ideal site – and as
well as hating cold, wet winter soil, it also dislikes hot, humid nights.
The leaves may discolour if attacked by rust, but this is no reason for
not growing it. During mild winters, the leaves remain evergreen,
adding colour to the winter garden, while in cold-climate gardens
you can cut off the foliage in the autumn. Spring is the best time
to divide clumps.

OTHER VARIETIES *E. canadensis* (taller-growing, blue-green leaves,
dense green flower spikes); *E. hispidus* (pale silvery-blue leaves).

PLANT PROFILE	
HEIGHT 15cm (6in)	
SPREAD 30cm (12in)	
SITE Full sun	
SOIL Free-draining	
HARDINESS Fully hardy	
FLOWERING Summer	

E

Eomecon chionantha Snow poppy

THE SNOW POPPY is nothing like a traditional poppy, largely because it is a quick-spreading, invasive perennial with kidney-shaped leaves up to 10cm (4in) wide. The white, four-petalled flowers have a yellow centre, and are individually attractive, although it needs hot weather in order to flower freely in the early summer. It makes good ground cover when grown on moist but free-draining soil that never dries out, even in summer – for example, on a shady bank or in a shrub border. The more fertile the soil, the more prolifically it will spread.

PLANT PROFILE

HEIGHT 40cm (16in)

SPREAD Indefinite

SITE Light shade or full sun

SOIL Fertile, moist but free-draining

HARDINESS Fully hardy

FLOWERING Late spring to midsummer

Epilobium angustifolium var. *album* Willow herb

E

THIS COTTAGE GARDEN FAVOURITE has spires of white flowers blooming above the foliage and makes a lively background to reds and bright blues. It quickly multiplies, creating large clumps, and spreads by seed and underground roots. You can stop willow herb from spreading excessively by cutting off the flowers as soon as they start to fade, thus eliminating the seed. You can also slice the roots with a spade and dig out any unwanted growth. Slugs and snails can attack the stems, but given its prolific nature, they never become a real problem. Willow herb likes moist but free-draining soil.

OTHER VARIETIES *E. dodonaei* (pinkish-purple flowers); *E. glabellum* (creamy-white or pink flowers).

PLANT PROFILE
HEIGHT To 1.5m (5ft)
SPREAD 1m (3ft)
SITE Full sun or partial shade
SOIL Moist but free-draining
HARDINESS Fully hardy
FLOWERING Midsummer to early autumn

E

Epimedium pinnatum subsp. *colchicum* Barrenwort

TINY, ALMOST ORCHID-LIKE FLOWERS, sometimes with long spurs, consisting of four, flat, oval, bright yellow petals grace this plant. The flowers range up the stems, above the dark, evergreen, heart-shaped leaves that form a large clump at the base. It thrives in rich soil under trees or near evergreen shrubs that provide shelter against cold winds. If grown in more open, sunnier ground, the soil needs to be covered with a thick mulch of compost to lock in moisture. Cut back the leaves in late winter or early spring.

OTHER VARIETIES *E. grandiflorum* (white, yellow, pink, or purple flowers); *E. x perralchicum* (larger-growing, bright yellow flowers); *E. x youngianum* 'Niveum' (pure white flowers).

PLANT PROFILE
HEIGHT 30–40cm (12–16in)
SPREAD 25cm (10in)
SITE Partial shade
SOIL Moist, fertile, free-draining
HARDINESS Fully hardy
FLOWERING Spring

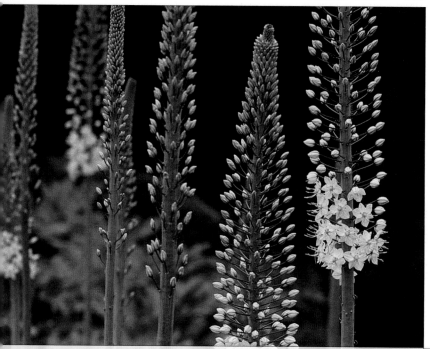

Eremurus robustus Foxtail lily

E

SPIRES OF TINY, PALE PINK FLOWERS make an eye-catching sight at the back of a border in a cottage-style or gravel garden. This is a tall eremurus and it associates well in the garden with the shorter types, such as the yellow *Eremurus stenophyllus* and white *E. himalaicus*. Foxtail lilies are quite fussy and demand fertile, free-draining soil and a warm, sheltered site. Staking is important to ensure the flower spires stand tall and erect, especially in exposed sites.

PLANT PROFILE
HEIGHT To 3m (10ft)
SPREAD To 1.2m (4ft)
SITE Full sun
SOIL Fertile, free-draining
HARDINESS Fully hardy
FLOWERING Early and midsummer

OTHER VARIETY *E.* x *isabellinus* 'Cleopatra' (orange flowers).

E

Erigeron 'Dunkelste Aller'

THESE COLOURFUL FLOWERS have a yellow centre and petals that are a rich, dark violet (in German, 'Dunkelste Aller' means 'darkest of all'). Given free-draining soil and some midday shade, it makes a strong show in early summer, but water well in prolonged periods of drought. It associates well with pink and white erigerons in a formal or cottage-style garden. Deadheading promotes extra flowers and division every three years maintains the plant's vigour.

OTHER VARIETIES *E.* 'Charity' (semi-double, lilac-pink flowers); *E.* 'Prosperity' (almost double, mauve-blue flowers); *E.* 'Quakeress' (pink-flushed white flowers); *E.* 'Wuppertal' (semi-double, dark-lilac flowers).

PLANT PROFILE

HEIGHT 60cm (24in)

SPREAD 45cm (18in)

SITE Full sun

SOIL Free-draining

HARDINESS Fully hardy

FLOWERING Early and midsummer

Eriophyllum lanatum Golden yarrow

THIS BRIGHT, FLASHY YELLOW PLANT is suitable for rock and gravel gardens, dry-stone walls, terraces and as edging at the front of a border. It is well worth growing if you can provide excellent drainage coupled with average-to-poor soil. The leaves are 8cm (3in) long, and stems are abundantly covered with open, daisy-like flowers with darker yellow eyes. Being drought-tolerant, it is easy to grow and invariably makes a fun display when planted in cracks in a patio. Take precautions against attacks from slugs and snails, and when growing golden yarrow in rock gardens, leave space for it to spread or it will soon swamp its neighbours.

PLANT PROFILE
HEIGHT 40cm (16in)
SPREAD 40cm (16in)
SITE Full sun
SOIL Average, free-draining
HARDINESS Fully hardy
FLOWERING Late spring to summer

| E | *Erodium chrysanthum* Heron's bill |

SIMILAR TO A GERANIUM (cranesbill), the flowers of this perennial give way to berries with a long beak, or bill. The summer-long flowers are pale yellow and blend beautifully with the attractive, silver-green leaves. Originally coming from rocky sites in Greece, it hates winter wet and requires gritty soil with excellent drainage. Grow it in a trough or rockery, raised bed, or gap in a terrace or patio paving. It can be potted up in the autumn and kept over winter in the greenhouse to prevent it from rotting in wet soil.

OTHER VARIETIES   *E. cheilanthifolium* (pale pink or white flowers with red veins); *E. corsicum* (rose-pink flowers with darker veins); *E. glandulosum* (lilac-pink flowers); *E. manescaui* (magenta-purple flowers).

PLANT PROFILE

HEIGHT 15cm (6in)

SPREAD 40cm (16in)

SITE Full sun

SOIL Fertile, free-draining

HARDINESS Fully hardy

FLOWERING Summer

Eryngium variifolium Sea holly

E

ARCHITECTURAL, QUIRKY AND FUN, there is a wide range of sea hollies, many with blue or silvery tints, and all with striking flowers. *Eryngium variifolium* forms a mass of sharp-tipped spines and must be kept away from the edge of a border where young children play, but position it where it can still be seen clearly. It is strange and shapely, with white-veined leaves at soil level, and stiff, branched stems. Ideal for coastal gardens with poor soil and sharp drainage, but it is not totally hardy and will need a warm, sheltered site in colder areas.

OTHER VARIETIES *E. bourgatii* (grey-green flowers); *E. bourgatii* 'Oxford Blue' (silvery-blue flowers); *E. giganteum* (taller-growing, steel-blue flowers); *E.* x *oliverianum* (bright silver-blue flowers).

PLANT PROFILE
HEIGHT 30–40cm (12–16in)
SPREAD 25cm (10in)
SITE Full sun
SOIL Free-draining
HARDINESS Frost hardy
FLOWERING Mid- and late summer

E

Erysimum 'Bowles Mauve' Wallflower

THRIVING HAPPILY IN THE CRACKS of a dry-stone wall, the common name of 'wallflower' is completely accurate. Adding colour and a sweet, pervasive scent, it is also a favourite for the front of a border or an island bed planted with spring bedding. The only problem is that it is very short-lived – four years with good luck and a very light, free-draining soil – but replacement cuttings are easy to take. There are many fine alternatives, in a range of colours from white to red, all of which create a lively display.

OTHER VARIETIES *E.* 'Bredon' (rich yellow flowers); *E. cheiri* 'Harpur Crewe' (double, yellow flowers); *E. linifolium* 'Variegatum' (mauve flowers, white-variegated leaves); *E.* 'Moonlight' (sulphur-yellow flowers).

PLANT PROFILE

HEIGHT 75cm (30in)

SPREAD 60cm (24in)

SITE Full sun

SOIL Free-draining

HARDINESS Fully hardy

FLOWERING Late winter to summer

Erythronium 'Pagoda' Dog's-tooth violet

E

A SUPERB SPRING PERENNIAL, 'Pagoda' has a combination of yellow flowers and bright green leaves. A delicate-looking beauty, it needs to be planted in front of, and shaded by, border shrubs in what equates to a woodland site. It likes moisture throughout the year, so don't let it bake over summer. Other good choices include *Erythronium dens-canis* with white, pink, or lilac flowers, and *E. revolutum* which has swept back pinky-white petals with a yellow centre.

OTHER VARIETIES *E. californicum* (creamy-white flowers with brownish-orange markings); *E. dens-canis* 'Pink Perfection' (clear pink flowers); *E. dens-canis* 'Snowflake' (pure white flowers); *E.* 'Kondo' (scented, lemon-yellow flowers); *E. tuolumnense* (bright yellow flowers).

PLANT PROFILE	
HEIGHT 15–35cm (6–14in)	
SPREAD 10cm (4in)	
SITE Partial shade	
SOIL Moist, fertile	
HARDINESS Fully hardy	
FLOWERING Spring	

E

Eupatorium purpureum subsp. *maculatum* 'Atropurpureum' Joe Pye weed

THIS BIG PLANT for a large border or wild garden looks its best in the second half of summer, when it forms massive clumps. Coming from damp sites in eastern North America, it also likes bog gardens and sites near streams and natural ponds. If being grown in borders, the soil must not bake dry or it will flop. The flowers attract bees and butterflies, and appear in flat clusters just above the foliage on stiff, purplish stems. Use this plant in bold groups with other late-summer big hitters, such as rudbeckias, which also like damp soil.

OTHER VARIETIES *E. album* 'Braunlaub' (brown-flushed leaves and flowers); *E. cannabinum* (smaller-growing, pink, purple, or white flowers); *E. rugosum* (pure white flowers).

PLANT PROFILE
HEIGHT 2.2m (7ft)
SPREAD 1m (3ft)
SITE Full sun or partial shade
SOIL Damp, fertile
HARDINESS Fully hardy
FLOWERING Midsummer to early autumn

Euphorbia dulcis 'Chameleon' Spurge

E

MAKE SURE YOU BUY 'Chameleon' rather than the parent, *Euphorbia dulcis*, as the former has marvellous purple foliage right through the summer which flares up even more in the autumn, making it one of the most eye-catching spurges. By cutting it back after flowering you can promote a second, fresh batch of leaves. Plant it at the front of a border or by a path, in moist, rich soil and some light shade. Wear gloves when handling or pruning because the sap can irritate the skin and eyes, and all parts of the plant are poisonous.

OTHER VARIETIES *E. amygdaloides* var. *robbiae* (leathery, dark green leaves); *E. griffithii* 'Fireglow' (orange-red bracts around flowerheads); *E. palustris* (bright green leaves, yellow bracts).

PLANT PROFILE	
HEIGHT 30cm (12in)	
SPREAD 30cm (12in)	
SITE Dappled shade	
SOIL Moist, fertile	
HARDINESS Fully hardy	
FLOWERING Early summer	

E

Euphorbia polychroma Spurge

AT ITS PEAK AT THE END OF SPRING, this evergreen spurge with its bright greeny-yellow bracts combines well with bright red tulips, and enlivens borders in the lull between the main spring show and early summer flowers. Its compact foliage makes an attractive low mound throughout the year, and in the autumn the foliage can display red and purple hues. This spurge is happy in a range of soils but does best in sun. Other good choices include 'Major' which grows slightly taller, and 'Candy' which has a purple tinge in spring. Wear gloves when handling spurge because the sap irritates the skin.

OTHER VARIETIES *E. dulcis* 'Chameleon' (purple leaves, yellow–green bracts); *E. griffithii* 'Dixter' (coopery dark green leaves, orange bracts).

PLANT PROFILE
HEIGHT 40cm (16in)
SPREAD 60cm (24in)
SITE Full sun
SOIL Moist, free-draining
HARDINESS Fully hardy
FLOWERING Mid-spring to midsummer

Ferula communis Giant fennel

F

THIS HIGHLY IMPRESSIVE BORDER PLANT should not be confused
with the fennel used for cooking. Its delightful, feathery leaves can
reach a huge 45cm (18in) in length, although there is a slow build-
up, possibly taking a couple of years, before the tall flower stems
topped by a scattering of yellow flowers make their appearance. It
is such a climactic performance that the plant may then die after
scattering new seed around, or take another couple of years to
flower again. Grow giant fennel in reasonably fertile, well-drained
soil in a sunny, protected site because it is not totally hardy. Protect
the crown of the plant with bracken over winter.

OTHER VARIETY *F. communis* subsp. *glauca* (blue flowers).

PLANT PROFILE

HEIGHT To 5m (15ft)

SPREAD 25–45cm
(10–18in)

SITE Full sun

SOIL Fertile

HARDINESS Frost hardy

FLOWERING Early and
midsummer

F

Festuca glauca 'Blaufuchs' Blue fescue

THE FLOWERS CANNOT COMPETE with the show of bright silver-blue, evergreen leaves that splay out to resemble the spines of a porcupine. Grow it in imaginative schemes, positioned at the front of a border, or alternating with other shapely plants in average to poor, free-draining soil. Mediterranean-type gardens are an ideal setting, alongside pots of unusual cacti. After a few years the foliage colour tends to fade, but dividing and replanting the vigorous outer portions will provide a fresh supply of plants.

OTHER VARIETIES *F. amethystina* (dense grey-green leaves); *F. eskia* (smaller-growing, rich green leaves); *F. valesiaca* 'Silbersee' (compact, pale silvery-blue leaves).

PLANT PROFILE	
HEIGHT To 30cm (12in)	
SPREAD 25cm (10in)	
SITE Sun	
SOIL Average, free-draining	
HARDINESS Fully hardy	
FLOWERING Early and midsummer	

Filipendula rubra 'Venusta' Queen of the prairie

F

THIS TALL, VIGOROUS SPREADER adds an attractive presence to bog gardens, the banks of streams, or wild gardens. The leafy red stems grow some 2m (6ft) high, with feathery flower plumes, similar in appearance to those of an astilbe, appearing just above them. This plant needs plenty of space, but if it spreads too far, slice off the snaking, shallow roots with a spade and dig out the excess growth. *Filipendula palmata* is more suitable for small gardens, reaching only 1.2m (4ft) high and 60cm (24in) wide.

OTHER VARIETIES *F. purpurea* (smaller-growing, carmine-red flowers); *F. ulmaria* (smaller-growing, creamy-white flowers); *F. vulgaris* 'Multiplex' (double creamy-white flowers from bronze buds).

PLANT PROFILE
HEIGHT 2–2.5m (6–8ft)
SPREAD 1.2m (4ft)
SITE Full sun or partial shade
SOIL Moist, free-draining
HARDINESS Fully hardy
FLOWERING Early and midsummer

F

Foeniculum vulgare 'Purpureum' Bronze fennel

THIS EXTREMELY USEFUL HERB can be grown in herb gardens or in borders, either right at the front, where it provides a see-through, feathery curtain of leaves or, because of its height, at the back where it can be seen clearly. It is an easy plant to grow and, although the soil should be free-draining, it tolerates heavier clay. The summer flowers are on the insipid yellow side, and can be snipped off to prevent self-seeding. While it can be grown as an ornamental plant, the leaves are also suitable for cooking. Pick and place them under a roast chicken where they lose their aniseed flavour and become quite nutty, enriching the juices. *Foeniculum vulgare* var. *dulce* (Florence fennel) is grown for its crisp, underground bulb which is used in stews and salads.

PLANT PROFILE
HEIGHT 1.8m (6ft)
SPREAD 45cm (18in)
SITE Full sun
SOIL Free-draining
HARDINESS Fully hardy
FLOWERING Summer

Fragaria 'Pink Panda' Strawberry

THIS IS NOT A FRUITING STRAWBERRY – there are better, more prolific alternatives with sweeter fruit. Rather, it is an ornamental, clump-forming, spreading plant with fresh green leaves and pink flowers. 'Pink Panda' makes an attractive edging plant, or it can be grown in gaps in a terrace or patio. New, young plants are attached to the parent by what looks like an umbilical cord – once the new plants are growing well, simply snip the cord and move them to your preferred position in the garden. If it becomes too invasive, clumps can be easily removed.

OTHER VARIETY *F. vesca* 'Variegata' (grey–green leaves with creamy–white markings).

PLANT PROFILE

HEIGHT 10–15cm (4–6in)

SPREAD 10–15cm (4–6in)

SITE Full sun or light dappled shade

SOIL Average, free-draining

HARDINESS Fully hardy

FLOWERING Late spring to mid-autumn

F | *Francoa sonchifolia*

THIS IS A HIGHLY ATTRACTIVE, intriguing plant. It makes rosettes of hairy, crinkled, bright green leaves that hug the ground, and sends up vertical spikes of tiny, pure pink flowers in midsummer. The flowers stay fresh for a long time, giving a beautiful border display. It needs free-draining soil because the roots will quickly rot if stuck in cold, wet, winter soil. And since it is not completely hardy, it also needs a warm, sunny situation. The best way to increase your stock of plants is to divide them in the spring – make sure that new plants are well watered until they are firmly rooted and established.

OTHER VARIETIES   *F. appendiculata* (pale pink flowers); *F. ramosa* (white flowers with pink markings).

PLANT PROFILE

HEIGHT 75cm (30in)

SPREAD 45cm (18in)

SITE Full sun or partial shade

SOIL Free-draining

HARDINESS Frost hardy

FLOWERING Midsummer

Gaillardia 'Kobold' Blanket flower

G

THE FLAMBOYANT, EXTRA LARGE, daisy-like flowers of this plant add fizz to any border. The round blooms have a prominent red disc in the middle, and the petals are red with yellow tips. Blanket flowers need average (not too rich), free-draining soil, and are reasonably drought-tolerant. The stems are quite floppy, however, and need to be supported by twiggy sticks so that the colourful petals are clearly visible. The blooms are good for cutting and will enliven any indoor display. Alternatives include 'Dazzler' and 'Wirral Flame' which are orange-red with yellow tips, and the wine-red 'Burgunder'.

OTHER VARIETY *G.* x *grandiflora* (taller-growing, flowers with yellow and red petals and yellow-brown centres).

PLANT PROFILE
HEIGHT 30cm (12in)
SPREAD 45cm (18in)
SITE Full sun
SOIL Average, free-draining
HARDINESS Fully hardy
FLOWERING Early summer to early autumn

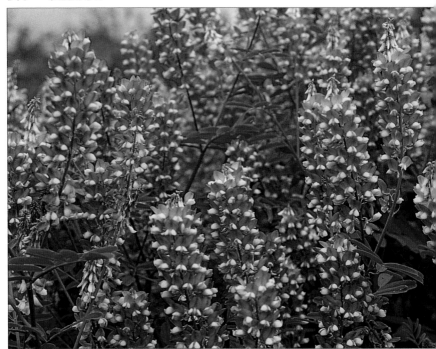

G | *Galega officinalis* Goat's rue

A COTTAGE GARDEN FAVOURITE, goat's rue forms a spread of pea-like flowers on scores of floppy spikes that require staking for a good display. Use it in borders to link different colour schemes, or to contrast with more upright, architectural plants. If growing the mauve form, it is worth mixing it with the white 'Alba'. Plants spread by seed, soon forming large clumps (to prevent this, nip off the fading flowers before they set seed). Quite unfussy, it will grow in most soils, from moist to dry, and tolerates light shade.

OTHER VARIETIES *G. x hartlandii* 'Lady Wilson' (bicoloured mauve-blue and white flowers); *G. orientalis* (blue-violet flowers).

PLANT PROFILE

HEIGHT 30cm–1.5m (1–5ft)

SPREAD 90cm (36in)

SITE Full sun or partial shade

SOIL Average

HARDINESS Fully hardy

FLOWERING Mid- and late summer

Galium odoratum Sweet woodruff

G

GIVEN PLENTY OF SUN at the edge of a wooded area, this attractive little plant will spread freely. The tiny flowers perch above bright green leaves and, after two or three years, it will make a beautiful ground-covering carpet, looking its best when the bluebells have finished their show. Ideally, the soil needs to be on the moist side and fertile. To increase your stock of new plants, divide and replant clumps in the early spring. Beware of planting sweet woodruff in borders because, although pretty, it is quite invasive and soon becomes a nuisance.

OTHER VARIETY   *G. verum* (narrow leaves, yellow flowers).

PLANT PROFILE	
HEIGHT 45cm (18in)	
SPREAD 45cm (18in)	
SITE Sun or partial shade	
SOIL Moist, fertile	
HARDINESS Fully hardy	
FLOWERING Late spring to midsummer	

G | *Gaura lindheimeri*

FROM A DISTANCE THE SMALL, WHITE, long-lasting flowers on top of the slender stems look like butterflies. Gaura is a bonus in formal borders and cottage gardens where it doesn't need copious watering in prolonged dry periods yet still performs well. Its 'fluttery' flowers and small leaves soften the scene when planted near a chunky shrub or a dominating feature. While small gardens are unlikely to need more than one plant, if you want more, it is very easy to propagate in the spring, whether by cuttings or division.

OTHER VARIETIES *G. lindheimeri* 'Corrie's Gold' (gold-margined leaves); *G. lindheimeri* 'Siskiyou Pink' (warm pink flowers); *G. lindheimeri* 'Whirling Butterflies' (smaller-growing, grey-green leaves, red flowers).

PLANT PROFILE

HEIGHT To 1.5m (5ft)

SPREAD 90cm (36in)

SITE Full sun

SOIL Free-draining

HARDINESS Fully hardy

FLOWERING Late spring to early autumn

Gentiana asclepiadea Willow gentian

G

IN ORDER TO SEE a good display of the 5cm (2in) long flowers, you must pander to the needs of this plant. The soil must be moist and rich, and mulched in spring with a thick layer of leaf mould. Plant the willow gentian on the shady side of a shrub or in light shade in a border. When it is growing well the flower stems tend to arch over, adding an informal note. Try to pick the right site at the outset because established plants dislike being moved. Shorter gentians, such as *Gentiana acaulis*, are good for the rock garden.

OTHER VARIETIES *G. asclepiadea* var. *alba* (green-tinged white flowers); *G.* 'Inverleith' (smaller-growing, intense pale blue flowers with darker stripes); *G. septemfida* (purplish-blue flowers).

PLANT PROFILE	
HEIGHT 60–90cm (24–36in)	
SPREAD 45cm (18in)	
SITE Light shade	
SOIL Moist, fertile	
HARDINESS Fully hardy	
FLOWERING Mid- or late summer to early autumn	

G

Geranium 'Johnson's Blue'

JUSTIFIABLY A BIG FAVOURITE, this perennial produces a prolific
display of saucer-shaped, lavender-blue flowers that lend themselves
to all manner of colour contrasts. Like any blue flower, when it is
seen in light shade the blue looks slightly darker than when in full
sun. After it has finished flowering, shear over the plant to produce a
fresh, neat clump of leaves. Geraniums grow in most soils, except for
extremes of dry and wet, and in sun or shade. There are also dozens
of varieties to choose from in the white-pink-purple-blue range.

OTHER VARIETIES   G. 'Ann Folkard' (magenta flowers veined with
black); *G. cinereum* 'Ballerina' (purplish-red flowers with darker veins).

PLANT PROFILE	
HEIGHT 30–45cm (12–18in)	
SPREAD 60–75cm (24–30in)	
SITE Full sun or partial shade	
SOIL Average, free-draining	
HARDINESS Fully hardy	
FLOWERING Summer	

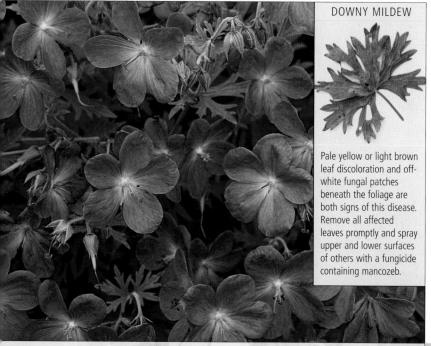

Geranium himalayense 'Plenum'

G

THIS LOW-GROWING GERANIUM has its main flush of violet-blue blooms – set against deeply cut, distinctively veined foliage – in early summer. Use its spreading, scrambling growth to advantage, letting it tumble over the edges of a straight path to soften and blur its line, or grow it beneath roses and in front of shrubs, where it will swamp any weeds. Geraniums are happy in most soils except for extremes of dry and wet, and will grow in full sun or shade.

OTHER VARIETIES *G. clarkei* 'Kashmir White' (white flowers with lilac-pink veins); *G. himalayense* 'Gravetye' (blue flowers shading into red at the centre); *G. renardii* (white to lavender flowers with violet veins).

PLANT PROFILE

HEIGHT 25cm (10in)

SPREAD 60cm (24in)

SITE Full sun or partial shade

SOIL Average, free-draining

HARDINESS Fully hardy

FLOWERING Early Summer

G

Geranium sanguineum Bloody cranesbill

THE COMMON NAME HERE comes from the fantastic clash of orange-, red-, and brown-tinted autumn foliage. The bloody cranesbill flowers over a long summer period, forming mats of deeply divided foliage and pretty cup-shaped, magenta-pink flowers. Grow this plant in rock and gravel gardens, gaps in paving, or as ground cover. It also makes a good edging for the front of a border or to line a pathway. Geraniums grow in most soils except for extremes of dry and wet, and are happy in sun or light shade.

OTHER VARIETIES *G. sanguineum* 'Album' (white flowers); *G. sanguineum* 'Elsbeth' (bright purple flowers); *G. sanguineum* 'Glenluce' (rose-pink flowers); *G. sanguineum* 'Max Frei' (magenta flowers).

PLANT PROFILE	
HEIGHT 20cm (8in)	
SPREAD 40cm (16in)	
SITE Sun or light shade	
SOIL Average, free-draining	
HARDINESS Fully hardy	
FLOWERING Summer	

Geum 'Lady Stratheden'

RELIABLY UPBEAT AND CHEERFUL, 'Lady Stratheden' flowers over an extended period from late spring, and mixes well with the bright red of *Geum* 'Mrs. J. Bradshaw', sometimes known as 'Fireball'. Use geums in conjunction with shrubs that have a shorter flowering period – perhaps the spring-flowering *Choisya ternata* – where they will provide a continuity of colour throughout the summer. Geums are happy in most soils apart from heavy, waterlogged clay; good drainage is an important factor, as is bright sun.

OTHER VARIETIES G. 'Coppertone' (smaller-growing, apricot flowers with red centres); G. 'Fire Opal' (taller-growing, semi-double, dark orange flowers); G. 'Lemon Drops' (smaller-growing, lemon-yellow flowers).

PLANT PROFILE
HEIGHT 40–60cm (16–24in)
SPREAD 60cm (24in)
SITE Full sun
SOIL Average, free-draining
HARDINESS Fully hardy
FLOWERING Late spring to summer

G | *Gillenia trifoliata* Bowman's root

A GENTLE SHOW OF PINKISH–WHITE FLOWERS appears in early summer, with each bloom looking like a butterfly having just landed on top of a red-tinted stem. The colour is enlivened by the red calyces (leaf-like structures at the base of the flower) and red autumn foliage. Bowman's root is an excellent addition to any border with slightly acid or even neutral soil that is moist but free-draining. It likes a bright position in the garden, but some shade is needed during the hottest part of the day. To increase your stock of plants, divide it in early spring or mid-autumn and immediately replant the new sections.

PLANT PROFILE

HEIGHT To 1m (3ft)

SPREAD 60cm (24in)

SITE Partial shade

SOIL Moist, free-draining

HARDINESS Frost hardy

FLOWERING Early summer

Gladiolus communis subsp. *byzantinus*

G

USEFUL IN ALL TYPES OF BORDER, this hardy plant produces a shock of magenta blooms in early summer that immediately grabs the attention. It has a brief flowering spell and should be positioned where other perennials can take over and hide its fading foliage later in the year. Although hardy, it grows best in soil with good drainage and needs the protection of a mulch of compost in winter. Other varieties are half hardy and need very sheltered sites, or they can be potted up and kept somewhere frost free in winter.

OTHER VARIETIES *G. callianthus* (white flowers, with purple-marked throats, in late summer); *G. cardinalis* (bright red flowers with a white flash); *G. tristis* (taller-growing, yellow or creamy-white flowers).

PLANT PROFILE
HEIGHT To 1m (3ft)
SPREAD 8cm (3in)
SITE Full sun
SOIL Free-draining
HARDINESS Fully hardy
FLOWERING Late spring to early summer

G | *Glaucidium palmatum*

THIS HIGHLY UNDERRATED, slow-growing, mauve-flowering plant is suitable for shady sites, such as you might find in a woodland garden or at the shady end of a border. It produces an attractive mix of light green crinkled leaves, about 20cm (8in) long, with jagged edges, and 8cm (3in) wide flowers with golden centres. Grow this plant in rich, cool, moist ground where there is shelter from winds that could damage its leaves. Beware of slug attacks in the spring which will mar the new season's growth.

OTHER VARIETY *G. palmatum* var. *leucanthum* (white flowers).

PLANT PROFILE
HEIGHT 45cm (18in)
SPREAD 45cm (18in)
SITE Partial to deep shade
SOIL Moist, fertile
HARDINESS Fully hardy
FLOWERING Late spring and early summer

Glaucium flavum Yellow horned poppy

AN EYE-CATCHING PERENNIAL which looks particularly fine when set against the stony ground of a gravel garden. The rosettes of large, almost cabbage-like fleshy leaves are blue-green with wavy margins. Although short-lived, it self-seeds readily, especially when grown on free-draining, average-to-poor soil. It can just about be included in a herb garden because the ancient Greeks reckoned it could 'purge the belly', while the leaves 'removed ulcers from sheep's eyes'.

OTHER VARIETIES *G. corniculatum* (smaller-growing, crimson-red to orange flowers); *G. grandiflorum* (smaller-growing, dark orange to crimson flowers).

PLANT PROFILE	
HEIGHT 30–90cm (12–36in)	
SPREAD To 45cm (18in)	
SITE Full sun	
SOIL Average, free-draining	
HARDINESS Fully hardy	
FLOWERING Summer	

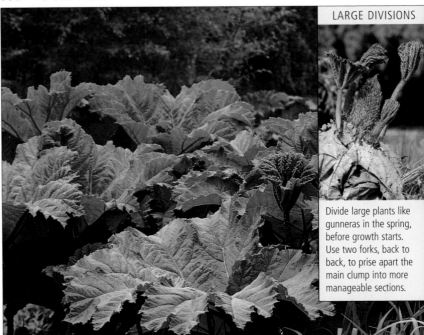

LARGE DIVISIONS

Divide large plants like gunneras in the spring, before growth starts. Use two forks, back to back, to prise apart the main clump into more manageable sections.

G | *Gunnera manicata*

THIS IS THE TOP CHOICE if you are looking for a magnificent pond-side plant but it definitely needs a large garden. Each spring *Gunnera manicata* produces fantastic, near vertical, prickly stems, and thick, oval leathery leaves, which are the largest on any hardy plant, growing up to 2m (6ft) wide. It is also possible to stand up straight under a gunnera without your head touching the foliage. The tiny flowers are packed on strange, cone-like structures under the leaves. The plant dies back in the autumn, when the leaves should be folded over the crown as protection. Provide moist soil and a sheltered site.

OTHER VARIETY *G. tinctoria* (smaller-growing, though still large).

PLANT PROFILE

HEIGHT 2.5m (8ft)

SPREAD 3.5m (11ft)

SITE Full sun or partial shade

SOIL Moist

HARDINESS Frost hardy

FLOWERING Early summer

Gypsophila 'Rosenschleier'

AIRY, OPEN SPRAYS of tiny white flowers (quickly turning pale pink) give this plant its other name of 'Rosy Veil'. Unlike the taller gypsophilas, it needs to be grown at the front of a border where it forms a dense mound of semi-evergreen leaves. Plant it on light, free-draining soil, and choose the right planting place at the outset because it dislikes disturbance. An alternative short gypsophila with pale pink flowers is *Gypsophila repens* 'Dorothy Teacher'.

OTHER VARIETIES *G. cerastioides* (smaller-growing, white flowers); *G. paniculata* 'Bristol Fairy' (taller-growing, double, white flowers); *G. paniculata* 'Compacta Plena' (double, soft pink to white flowers).

PLANT PROFILE
HEIGHT 40–50cm (16–20in)
SPREAD 1m (3ft)
SITE Full sun
SOIL Free-draining
HARDINESS Fully hardy
FLOWERING Mid- and late summer

H | *Hacquetia epipactis*

THIS FUN, QUIRKY LITTLE PLANT is ideal for any moist, shady parts of the garden. The clusters of tiny yellow flowers, which gradually turn green, are surrounded by a ring of bright green petal-like bracts, and these are followed soon after by the appearance of the oval leaves. *Hacquetia epipactis* can be grown in rock gardens where its low mounds are ideally suited to the scale of planting. It also provides a good partner to plants such as hostas, which enjoy the same site and soil conditions. Look out for slugs and snails in spring, as they will quickly demolish the new growth.

PLANT PROFILE

HEIGHT 15cm (6in)

SPREAD 23cm (9in)

SITE Partial shade

SOIL Moist

HARDINESS Fully hardy

FLOWERING Late winter and early spring

Hakonechloa macra 'Aureola'

H

THIS HIGH-PERFORMANCE GRASS is grown chiefly for its fountain of 25cm (10in) long, bright yellow- and green-striped leaves. It hits a high note from the moment the foliage starts to appear in spring; come autumn, the leaves take on a red tinge that persists into winter. 'Aureola' makes a satisfying oval shape, and can be used as a feature plant in a pot, to highlight the front of a border, or to fringe a pond. It can also be grown in rows, softening the edges of a path, and in formal, geometric gardens interspersed with clipped box (*Buxus*) plants. The pale green flowers (*see inset*) appear from late summer to early autumn.

PLANT PROFILE

HEIGHT 35cm (14in)

SPREAD 40cm (16in)

SITE Full sun or partial shade

SOIL Moist, fertile, free-draining

HARDINESS Fully hardy

FLOWERING Late summer to mid-autumn

H | *Hedychium densiflorum* Ginger lily

SHOWY, SHAPELY, GLOSSY LEAVES, up to 40cm (16in) long and, in the summer, a short stem packed with tiny flowers radiating right the way around, are the key features of this dramatic plant. Most gardens have a slightly shady, sheltered spot, with moist but free-draining soil, and that's all it takes to grow this richly scented Himalayan perennial (shelter is important because it is not totally hardy). Without these conditions it can be grown in a large pot. An even showier alternative is the scented *Hedychium gardnerianum*.

OTHER VARIETIES *H. coccineum* (smaller-growing, pale to deep red, orange, pink, or white flowers); *H. densiflorum* 'Assam Orange' (densely borne, deep orange flowers).

PLANT PROFILE	
HEIGHT To 5m (15ft)	
SPREAD 2m (6ft)	
SITE Sun or partial shade	
SOIL Fertile, moist but free-draining	
HARDINESS Frost hardy	
FLOWERING Late summer	

Helenium 'Moerheim Beauty' Sneezeweed

H

THESE KEY PLANTS for the summer border have an arresting show of large, daisy-like, orange-red and yellow flowers. Those of 'Moerheim Beauty' have coppery-red blooms and the typical, highly distinctive central eye – in this case, dark brown. It makes a perfect background plant for drifts of fiery reds and oranges, and its long flowering season extends from the start to the end of summer. Not too fussy, it will thrive in most soils with decent drainage but not dry, baked conditions. It is a sturdy grower and does not need staking.

OTHER VARIETIES *H*. 'Bruno' (taller-growing, deep crimson flowers); *H*. 'Goldfuchs' (tawny-orange flowers); *H*. 'Wyndley' (yellow flowers overlaid with dark orange).

PLANT PROFILE

HEIGHT 90cm (36in)

SPREAD 60cm (24in)

SITE Full sun

SOIL Moist

HARDINESS Fully hardy

FLOWERING Early to late summer

H

Helianthus 'Lemon Queen' Sunflower

NOT ALL SUNFLOWERS are giant annuals with satellite-dish, brash yellow heads – 'Lemon Queen' has soft, pale yellow, small flowers, about 10cm (4in) wide, with a darker yellow eye. It is a bushy performer for late summer with an abundant supply of blooms, but needs support to stop it flopping. Adding a cheery touch to cottage gardens, you can also grow a row of them as an internal hedge, with clematis and nasturtiums sprinting through the stems. Provide fertile, moist but free-draining soil.

OTHER VARIETIES *H.* 'Capenoch Star' (lemon-yellow flowers); *H.* 'Loddon Gold' (double, rich yellow flowers); *H.* 'Monarch' (semi-double, yellow-brown flowers); *H. salicifolius* (taller-growing, gold flowers).

PLANT PROFILE

HEIGHT 1.7m (5½ft)

SPREAD 1.2m (4ft)

SITE Full sun

SOIL Fertile, moist but free-draining

HARDINESS Fully hardy

FLOWERING Summer

Helichrysum 'Schwefellicht'

H

SMALL, FLUFFY, SULPHUR–YELLOW FLOWERS that turn orange-yellow, held on white, woolly stems, create an attractive display in late summer. This helichrysum can be grown at the front of a border, in raised beds or in a Mediterranean-style or gravel garden where it combines well with lavenders and the shorter varieties of red hot poker (*Kniphofia*). Excellent drainage is vital for this plant to thrive, while the soil can vary from poor to average. Most of the good alternatives are shrubs, such as *Helichrysum petiolare* and *H. splendidum*, but there is a smaller white-flowering perennial available.

OTHER VARIETY *H. milfordiae* (smaller-growing, white flowers).

PLANT PROFILE	
HEIGHT 40cm (16in)	
SPREAD 30cm (12in)	
SITE Full sun	
SOIL Average, free-draining	
HARDINESS Fully hardy	
FLOWERING Late summer	

H | *Helictotrichon sempervirens*

THE SUMMER–FLOWERING STEMS of this smart-looking, bristling grass shoot high above its near-vertical, narrow, grey-blue leaves. It is a beautiful, graceful plant when in bloom, and adds great charm to any gravel garden or border, where the tall flower stems will stand out best when set against a dark background. The soil needs to be free-draining and preferably on the poor side. Leave it unpruned over winter, and cut it back in the early spring. Comb out old, dead leaves with your splayed fingers, but beware of the sharp tips which can cut your skin.

OTHER VARIETY *H. sempervirens* 'Saphirsprudel' (more vigorous, broader leaves).

PLANT PROFILE
HEIGHT To 1.35m (4½ft)
SPREAD 60cm (24in)
SITE Full sun
SOIL Poor, free-draining
HARDINESS Fully hardy
FLOWERING Early and midsummer

Heliopsis helianthoides var. *scabra* 'Sommersonne' Ox eye

H

THE BRACING, GOLDEN-YELLOW, daisy-like flowers of the ox eye last right through the summer. Sometimes known as the false sunflower because of the similarity in flower shape, it looks good when grown in drifts, but never plant it next to a gentle pastel colour or it will hog the limelight. It requires minimum care, does not need regular feeding or watering, and thrives in most soils, even quite poor ones. It makes bushy clumps, but needs some support to keep the stems erect especially in exposed windy gardens.

OTHER VARIETIES *H. helianthoides* var. *scabra* 'Goldgefieder' (taller-growing, double, golden-yellow flowers); *H. helianthoides* var. *scabra* 'Goldgrünherz' (double, lemon-yellow flowers).

PLANT PROFILE
HEIGHT 90cm (36in)
SPREAD 60cm (24in)
SITE Full sun
SOIL Average
HARDINESS Fully hardy
FLOWERING Midsummer to early autumn

LEAF BLOTCH

All hellebores are prone to this problem, in which grey-brown blotches are seen on leaves and stems. Remove all affected parts at once and new leaves should soon regenerate.

H | *Helleborus* x *sternii* **Hellebore**

IT IS IMPOSSIBLE TO TELL which of its parents this hellebore will most resemble. It can sometimes look more like the hardy *Helleborus argutifolius*, with its tough, toothed leaves and white flowers, or the smaller *H. lividus*, with pink-flushed blooms. Either way, it is trouble free and generally has pinkish-purple flushed flowers. The two best-known types are 'Boughton Beauty' (often closer to *H. argutifolius*), which has greenish flowers, pinkish-purple on the outside, and 'Blackthorn' (smaller, like *H. lividus*), with pink-tinged green flowers and unusual veined foliage. Both need shelter from cold winds.

OTHER VARIETIES *H. foetidus* (taller, purple-edged green flowers); *H. niger* (white, or pink-flushed flowers, on purple-marked stems).

PLANT PROFILE

HEIGHT 30–35cm (12–14in)

SPREAD 30cm (12in)

SITE Full sun or dappled shade

SOIL Moist, free-draining

HARDINESS Fully hardy

FLOWERING Late winter to mid-spring

Hemerocallis 'Stafford' Daylily

H

WITH A REGULAR SUCCESSION of flowers, each lasting a day, 'Stafford' is a typical daylily. It has enormous possibilities in the border, adding colour when early summer performers take a rest, or in a lively scheme with bright, hot colours. Daylilies need fertile, moist soil with plenty of well-rotted compost in the spring. Plants must be kept well watered from spring onwards and perform well in a sunny site. There are scores of daylilies on offer, in colours ranging from white to yellow, orange, lavender-blue, purple, and rich, dark red.

OTHER VARIETIES *H.* 'Green Flutter' (light yellow flowers with green-tinted throats); *H.* 'Stella de Oro' (bright yellow flowers).

PLANT PROFILE	
HEIGHT 70cm (28in)	
SPREAD 1m (3ft)	
SITE Full sun	
SOIL Moist, fertile	
HARDINESS Fully hardy	
FLOWERING Midsummer	

H | *Hepatica nobilis*

TYPICALLY GROWN BENEATH TREES, on the shady side of a shrub, or in pots in shady corners, this plant is an attractive addition to the spring garden. The open blue flowers, held above the leaves on top of thin stalks, may even start to bloom in late winter. Choose the right position from the outset because it dislikes being moved once in the ground. The soil must be rich and moist, the heavier the better, but not boggy. You can divide clumps in spring, but the divisions tend to take their time to become fully established.

OTHER VARIETIES *H. acutiloba* (smaller-growing, blue, pink, or white flowers); *H.* x *media* 'Ballardii' (taller-growing, deep blue flowers); *H. transsilvanica* (taller-growing, blue, white, or pale pink flowers).

PLANT PROFILE

HEIGHT 10cm (4in)

SPREAD 15cm (6in)

SITE Partial shade

SOIL Fertile, moist but free-draining

HARDINESS Fully hardy

FLOWERING Early spring

Hesperis matronalis var. *albiflora* Sweet rocket

H

THIS ESSENTIAL, EASY-GOING, and sweetly scented (especially in
the evening) plant adds a quiet, gentle, unforced touch to the late-
spring garden. It should be grown with the lilac or purple kinds
(*Hesperis matronalis*), and planted among spring-flowering shrubs
or bulbs for a colourful, perfumed display. Although short-lived,
rarely surviving more than three years, it self-seeds prolifically. Look
for seedlings close to the parent plant in the spring, and move them
to other sites in the garden. Dappled shade and poor soil are the
basic requirements.

OTHER VARIETIES *H. matronalis* (lilac or purple flowers);
H. matronalis var. *albiflora* 'Alba Plena' (double, white flowers).

PLANT PROFILE	
HEIGHT 90cm (36in)	
SPREAD 45cm (18in)	
SITE Sun or partial shade	
SOIL Poor, free-draining	
HARDINESS Fully hardy	
FLOWERING Late spring to midsummer	

H | *Heuchera* 'Chocolate Ruffles'

THE NEW HEUCHERAS have highly attractive winter leaves – those of 'Chocolate Ruffles', for example, are rich brown and purple beneath with ruffled edges. The small, purplish flowers are held on thin, bare stems, giving an airy, dainty appearance. Other good choices include 'Pewter Moon' with silver markings on the leaves and pale pink flowers, and *Heuchera micrantha* var. *diversifolia* 'Palace Purple' with bronze-red, jagged-edged foliage, and greenish-cream flowers. All like rich, moist but free-draining soil, and a sunny or shaded site.

OTHER VARIETIES *H.* 'Cascade Dawn' (red-purple leaves with pewter markings); *H.* 'Red Spangles' (smaller-growing, scarlet-crimson flowers throughout summer).

PLANT PROFILE
HEIGHT 75cm (30in)
SPREAD 40cm (16in)
SITE Sun or light shade
SOIL Moist, fertile, free-draining
HARDINESS Fully hardy
FLOWERING Early summer

x *Heucherella alba* 'Bridget Bloom'

H

LUSH, EVERGREEN, LOBED FOLIAGE for cottage gardens and borders is the key attraction of this plant. It has airy sprays of tiny pink and white flowers held on slim spires above the leaves. The foliage grows to 10cm (4in) long, and initially has brown marbling, turning bronze in the autumn. For the best results, provide partial shade and free-draining soil, which can be slightly acid. 'Bridget Bloom' combines well with asters, white geraniums and heucheras.

OTHER VARIETIES x *H. alba* 'Rosalie' (veined green leaves with a darker centre and pink flowers); x *H. tiarelloides* (larger-growing, tiny pink flowers on brownish-red stems from mid-spring to early summer).

PLANT PROFILE

HEIGHT To 40cm (16in)

SPREAD 30cm (12in)

SITE Sun or partial shade

SOIL Fertile, free-draining

HARDINESS Fully hardy

FLOWERING Late spring to mid-autumn

| H | *Hordeum jubatum* Squirrel tail grass |

THIS BEAUTIFUL SMALL GRASS has silky, silvery plumes, often tinged with purple at the top, that sway gracefully when caught by even the slightest breeze. Toward the end of summer the plumes turn beige. This versatile grass can be used in all manner of ways – ideas include planting it *en masse* to cover a small bed, with several strategically placed feature plants rising out of it, or using it to edge the front of a border. Although *Hordeum jubatum* is extremely short-lived, this is not a problem because it is a prolific self-seeder. In the spring, delay weeding – what look like small clumps of lawn grass in the border may, in fact, be young plants.

PLANT PROFILE

HEIGHT 50cm (20in)

SPREAD 30cm (12in)

SITE Full sun

SOIL Fertile, free-draining

HARDINESS Fully hardy

FLOWERING Early and midsummer

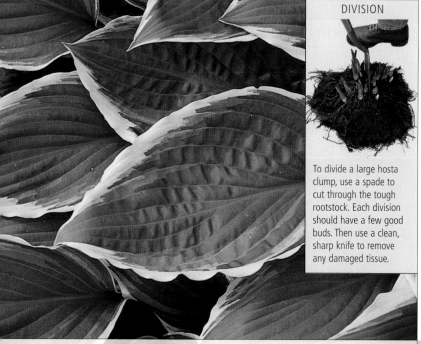

DIVISION

To divide a large hosta clump, use a spade to cut through the tough rootstock. Each division should have a few good buds. Then use a clean, sharp knife to remove any damaged tissue.

Hosta undulata var. *albomarginata*

H

THIS LARGE, SHOWY HOSTA has 18cm (7in) long leaves, each with a distinct white rim, and funnel-shaped mauve summer flowers on tall stems. It is an excellent plant for a damp, shady site and is a good performer in a border or in an attractive, large pot. This is just one of a huge variety of hostas that range in colour from yellow-green leaves ('September Sun') or bluish leaves ('Halcyon'), to those with dashy white margins ('Francee'). All hostas can suffer badly from slug damage, so take precautions – piling sharp grit around the stems may deter them and it also helps to highlight the foliage.

OTHER VARIETIES *H.* 'Frances Williams' (blue-green leaves, wide green-yellow margins); *H.* 'Patriot' (olive-green leaves, white margins).

PLANT PROFILE	
HEIGHT 55cm (22in)	
SPREAD 90cm (36in)	
SITE Full or partial shade	
SOIL Moist, fertile	
HARDINESS Fully hardy	
FLOWERING Summer	

H | *Houttuynia cordata* 'Chameleon'

DAMP, SHADY PLACES in the Far East are home to the parent of this plant – precisely the same conditions that 'Chameleon' needs in the garden. Its smartly marked leaves have patches of dark pinky-red, green and cream, but it needs bright light rather than shade for the colouring to become really vivid. It is tempting to plant it in the border, but do so at your peril – it's a notorious invader and is far better used as ground cover. Insert paving slabs or slate vertically around the walls of its planting hole, creating a lined square or rectangular pit, to curtail its spreading roots.

OTHER VARIETY *H. cordata* 'Flore Pleno' (leaves variegated in green, pale yellow, and red, flowers surrounded by white bracts).

PLANT PROFILE
HEIGHT To 30cm (12in)
SPREAD Indefinite
SITE Full sun or dappled shade
SOIL Moist
HARDINESS Fully hardy
FLOWERING Spring

Hypericum perforatum St. John's wort

H

USED BY HERBALISTS FOR CENTURIES, all you need to appreciate the bright yellow flowers of this plant is a border or herb garden with average soil. A multi-purpose herb, it oozes an anti-depressant red dye when mixed with alcohol, and a yellow dye when mixed with alum. Medicinally, it is said to cure just about everything – from burns and tennis elbow to shingles and sciatica – and it's often used in oils and tinctures. Use it only with professional guidance, however; eating it can cause a variety of severe effects, particularly lesions on white skin when exposed to sunlight. The word 'wort' originally meant root, herb, or plant.

OTHER VARIETY *H. orientale* (smaller-growing, golden-yellow flowers).

PLANT PROFILE

HEIGHT 60–110cm (24–42in)

SPREAD To 60cm (24in)

SITE Full sun

SOIL Average, free-draining

HARDINESS Fully hardy

FLOWERING Midsummer to mid-autumn

I

Imperata cylindrica 'Rubra' Japanese blood grass

HARD TO IGNORE, this flashy grass starts off red at the tip and then slowly 'burns' down until virtually the whole blade is a rich red colour. The silvery flowers make a good contrast with the foliage, but they appear only in long, hot summers. It can be used in a wide range of situations: at the front of a border, edging paths, around artificial ponds and, for a shocking contrast, in a white-themed garden. Unfortunately it dies back in winter, when it needs cutting to the ground and, because it is on the tender side, a thick winter mulch of compost to protect the roots. This warning is particularly relevant to young plants. It hates wet soil, and will flourish when growing in free-draining conditions in sun or light shade.

PLANT PROFILE	
HEIGHT	40cm (16in)
SPREAD	30cm (12in)
SITE	Sun or light shade
SOIL	Fertile, free-draining
HARDINESS	Frost hardy
FLOWERING	Late summer

Incarvillea delavayi

I

REMARKABLY EXOTIC YET EASY TO GROW, the rich-coloured flower trumpets of this plant have a yellow throat and are borne on top of erect stems, well clear of the leaves at the base. It likes free-draining, fertile soil that does not bake dry over summer. Because it hates sitting in soaking wet soil, plant it just under the soil surface and protect it over winter with a thick mulch of compost. The exotic flowers make it tempting to try growing other incarvilleas, but this one is the most popular because it is so reliable.

OTHER VARIETY *I. mairei* (purple-crimson flowers with white-striped purple on the lower lobes).

PLANT PROFILE	
HEIGHT 60cm (24in)	
SPREAD 30cm (12in)	
SITE Full sun, light shade	
SOIL Fertile, free-draining	
HARDINESS Fully hardy	
FLOWERING Early and midsummer	

I

Inula hookeri

THIS HARDY DAISY IS A ROBUST PLANT, with pale yellow flowers up to 8cm (3in) wide, the spidery petals of which shoot out from the inner brownish-yellow disc. The whole plant can be slightly invasive in ideal conditions, but the roots are easily sliced with a spade and the excess growth dug out. If space permits, try *Inula magnifica* which is the largest species available, growing up to 2m (6ft) high and 1m (3ft) wide. The flowers are golden-yellow, and it definitely needs a place at the back of a border.

OTHER VARIETIES *I. ensifolia* (smaller-growing, golden-yellow flowers); *I. helenium* (taller-growing, bright yellow flowers); *I. orientalis* (orange-yellow flowers); *I. racemosa* (taller-growing, light yellow flowers).

PLANT PROFILE

HEIGHT 60–75cm (24–30in)

SPREAD 60cm (24in)

SITE Partial shade

SOIL Moist, fertile, free-draining

HARDINESS Fully hardy

FLOWERING Late summer to mid-autumn

Iris pallida 'Variegata'

I

With its semi-evergreen leaves thrusting out of the soil like swords, this is a first-rate, highly versatile, spreading border iris. The foliage is bright green with a golden-yellow stripe, and the plant makes a strong architectural statement. The late spring and early summer flowers are soft blue. Use it to line a path or in a border or gravel garden interspersed with tall alliums or late-flowering tulips. *Iris pallida* 'Argentea Variegata' is equally attractive, though less vigorous, with silvery-white striped leaves. Both irises need free-draining soil and a sunny situation to thrive.

OTHER VARIETY *I. laevigata* 'Variegata' (smaller-growing, pale purple-blue flowers in summer, white- and green-striped leaves).

PLANT PROFILE
HEIGHT To 1.2m (4ft)
SPREAD Indefinite
SITE Sun
SOIL Fertile, free-draining
HARDINESS Fully hardy
FLOWERING Late spring and early summer

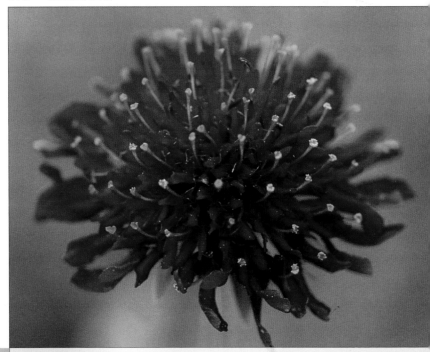

K | *Knautia macedonica*

WITH ITS LONG, THIN, WIRY STEMS and small, roundish, dark red pincushion flowers on top, this plant always catches the eye. It is more of a combination plant than a feature, and needs to be placed where the flowers stand out against, and poke through, the yellows and whites of adjacent plants. These neighbours should also provide some support for its floppy stems; if they're not suitable, push in twiggy sticks to prop up the plant. *Knautia macedonica* will survive in heavy soil but ideally prefers free-draining ground. Further plants can be raised easily from cuttings taken in the spring.

OTHER VARIETY *K. arvensis* (taller-growing, bluish-lilac, flat-topped flowers, dull green leaves).

PLANT PROFILE

HEIGHT To 80cm (32in)

SPREAD 45cm (18in)

SITE Full sun

SOIL Free-draining

HARDINESS Fully hardy

FLOWERING Mid- and late summer

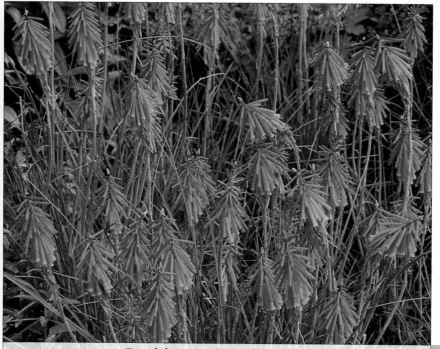

Kniphofia triangularis Red hot poker

K

EVERY GARDEN NEEDS a group of these clump-forming red hot pokers. The plant has club-like stems packed with tiny flowers at the top. *Kniphofia triangularis* is excellent in lively gravel gardens and end-of-season borders with asters, dahlias, fuchsias, hedychiums, and rudbeckias. Other flashy choices include the bright red 'Erecta', 'Mount Etna' (with scarlet buds and greenish-yellow flowers), *K. rooperi* (with orange-red flowers turning orange-yellow), and scarlet 'Samuel's Sensation'. Plant them in moist but free-draining soil.

OTHER VARIETIES *K. caulescens* (taller-growing, coral-red flowers fading to pale yellow); *K.* 'Little Maid' (smaller-growing, pale yellow flowers); *K.* 'Sunningdale Yellow' (long-lasting yellow flowers).

PLANT PROFILE
HEIGHT 60–90cm (24–36in)
SPREAD 45cm (18in)
SITE Sun or partial shade
SOIL Fertile, moist but free-draining
HARDINESS Fully hardy
FLOWERING Early and mid-autumn

K

Koeleria glauca Glaucous hair grass

GROWING IN THE WILD on sandy soil in Europe and Asia, glaucous hair grass makes a semi-evergreen upright clump with 20cm (8in) long, blue-tinged, grey-green leaves. The flowers appear slightly earlier than on many grasses. It is a valuable ingredient in a gravel garden, and makes an interesting edge to a border. Plant it in soil with excellent drainage, and because it declines in vigour in just a few growing seasons, you should dig up clumps and divide them every two years in the spring. Save the younger, more vigorous outer sections for replanting.

OTHER VARIETY *K. macrantha* (green foliage).

PLANT PROFILE

HEIGHT To 40cm (16in)

SPREAD 30cm (12in)

SITE Full sun or light shade

SOIL Free-draining

HARDINESS Fully hardy

FLOWERING Early and midsummer

Lamium maculatum 'White Nancy' Dead nettle

L

LOW-GROWING AND SEMI-EVERGREEN, this ground-cover plant spreads vigorously. The tiny silver leaves have a green rim, and the nettle-like flowers are small and bright white. It makes excellent ground cover for shady sites, or use it to decorate winter containers on a sheltered patio. Other types produce pink, purple, and red flowers. The best non-invasive dead nettles are the pink to white *Lamium armenum*, and the 60cm (24in) high, pinkish-purple *L. orvala*.

OTHER VARIETIES *L. maculatum* 'Aureum' (pink flowers, yellow leaves with paler centres); *L. maculatum* 'Beacon Silver' (pale pink flowers, green-margined silver leaves); *L. maculatum* 'Red Nancy' (purplish-red flowers); *L. orvala* 'Album' (taller-growing, pinkish-purple flowers).

PLANT PROFILE		
HEIGHT 15cm (6in)		
SPREAD To 1m (3ft) or more		
SITE Partial or deep shade		
SOIL Moist, free-draining		
HARDINESS Fully hardy		
FLOWERING Summer		

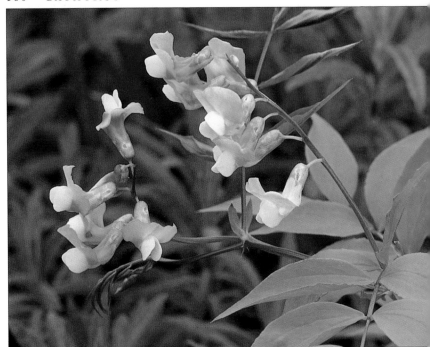

L

Lathyrus vernus 'Alboroseus' Spring vetchling

TYPICALLY GROWN AT THE FRONT of a border, in rock gardens or
even in woodland areas, spring vetchling is used for its early pink
and white flowers (unlike *Lathyrus vernus* which has purple flowers).
It makes dense growth with upright stems and lush green foliage,
and needs free-draining soil, although it's perfectly happy in poor
ground. However, it dislikes being dug up and planted in new sites,
so try to find the right position from the outset. For climbing,
scented, annual sweet peas, look for varieties of *L. odoratus*.

OTHER VARIETY *L. aureus* (taller-growing, yellow-orange flowers
from late spring to early summer, dark green leaves).

PLANT PROFILE	
HEIGHT 20–45cm (8–18in)	
SPREAD 45cm (18in)	
SITE Full sun or light shade	
SOIL Free-draining	
HARDINESS Fully hardy	
FLOWERING Spring	

Lavatera maritima Mallow

L

GIVING A SUBTLE END-OF-SEASON SHOW, this form of perennial mallow produces pink, lilac-pink, or even white flowers, 2.5cm (1in) wide. The growth is upright and quite shrubby, leading some to regard it as a shrub. Plant it in free-draining soil and provide some shelter from the damaging effects of icy winds. It thrives in coastal gardens where it is reliably evergreen. There are many other excellent mallows for midsummer flowers, including the perennial 'Bressingham Pink' and the shrubby, red-eyed, white 'Barnsley'.

OTHER VARIETIES *L. cachemiriana* (taller-growing, rose-pink flowers); *L.* x *clementii* 'Shorty' (smaller-growing, white or rose-pink flowers); *L. thuringiaca* (taller-growing, purple-pink flowers).

PLANT PROFILE	
HEIGHT	1.5m (5ft)
SPREAD	1m (3ft)
SITE	Full sun
SOIL	Free-draining
HARDINESS	Frost hardy
FLOWERING	Late summer to mid-autumn

L

Lespedeza thunbergii Bush clover

THIS SURPRISINGLY UNDERRATED plant provides an eye-catching contrast when planted with big, bold dahlias. It has delicate, small, beautifully formed purple-pink flowers on arching stems, and the leaves are small and oval. The display does not last that long – about two weeks – but the bush clover is well worth including in a bed or border, as there is little else in early autumn quite like it. Provide light, free-draining soil; in heavier clay, growth will be much slower. Despite its shrubby appearance, it doesn't need pruning because winter frosts will cut it back, although it reliably reshoots from soil level the following spring.

OTHER VARIETY *L. bicolor* (purple-pink flowers).

PLANT PROFILE	
HEIGHT	2m (6ft)
SPREAD	3m (10ft)
SITE	Full sun
SOIL	Free-draining
HARDINESS	Fully hardy
FLOWERING	Early autumn

Leucanthemum x *superbum* 'Wirral Supreme' Shasta daisy

L

EACH SUMMER THE SHASTA DAISIES can be relied on to give a good show. Robust and clump-forming, they have flowers with an outer ring of petals and a central eye. The blooms of 'Wirral Supreme' have a yellow eye, with a double row of white petals, and are held on long thin stems above dark green leaves. For a slightly more eccentric display, try 'Phyllis Smith' which has long, thin, twisty petals. Both may need staking, and will thrive in sun or a little shade in gardens with moist but free-draining soil.

OTHER VARIETIES *L.* x *superbum* 'Aglaia' (shorter, with semi–double white flowers); *L.* x *superbum* 'Esther Read' (double, white flowers); *L.* x *superbum* 'Silberprinzesschen' (shorter, with single white flowers).

PLANT PROFILE
HEIGHT 75cm (30in)
SPREAD 75cm (30in)
SITE Full sun or partial shade
SOIL Moist but free-draining
HARDINESS Fully hardy
FLOWERING Early summer to early autumn

L | *Leymus arenarius* Lyme grass

IN THE WILD IN NORTHERN EUROPE this grass is used to bind and stabilize sand dunes, but its chief value in gardens is its blue-grey, 60cm (24in) high leaves. Cut back the foliage after flowering and you will be rewarded with a fresh flush of colourful leaves to give a strong show in the autumn. Plant lyme grass in free-draining soil that's on the poor side. When happy, this drought-tolerant plant is a robust spreader but it can be contained by planting it in a spacious hole lined with paving slabs. After a few years the clump will need to be dug up, thinned out and replanted. The long, thin, graceful, blue-grey flower spikes can be used in displays of cut flowers.

PLANT PROFILE	
HEIGHT	1.5m (5ft)
SPREAD	Indefinite
SITE	Full sun
SOIL	Poor, free-draining
HARDINESS	Fully hardy
FLOWERING	Summer

Liatris spicata Gayfeather

THIS LATE-SUMMER PLANT is useful for a hot spot in a border with
moist but free-draining soil. Its stems stand smartly upright, at about
shoulder height, and are covered with clusters of tiny pink-purple
or white flowers that open and fade gradually in succession from
top to bottom. Other types offer various colours: 'Snow Queen'
and 'Floristan Weiss' (white), 'Blue Bird' (blue-purple), and 'Kobold'
(deep purple). Avoid growing gayfeather in heavy, water-retentive
clay or it will die in its first winter.

OTHER VARIETY *L. pycnostachya* (bright purple flowers in dense
spikes from midsummer).

PLANT PROFILE
HEIGHT 1.5m (5ft)
SPREAD 45cm (18in)
SITE Full sun
SOIL Moist but free-draining
HARDINESS Fully hardy
FLOWERING Late summer and early autumn

L | *Libertia grandiflora*

ADDING INTEREST TO LATE SPRING GARDENS, this evergreen, clump-forming plant sends up stems covered with sprays of small, white flowers above strap-shaped foliage that can reach 75cm (30in) in length. *Libertia formosa* is very similar and is a good alternative plant. Both are borderline hardy and need a thick, protective mulch of compost over winter, especially in their first few years, until they're well established. As an option, you can plant them in a sheltered, warm site – for example, at the base of a sunny wall. Rich, moist soil with good drainage is required.

OTHER VARIETIES *L. caerulescens* (smaller-growing, pale blue flowers); *L. ixioides* (smaller-growing, white flowers with brown or green).

PLANT PROFILE

HEIGHT To 90cm (36in)

SPREAD 60cm (24in)

SITE Full sun

SOIL Moist, fertile, free-draining

HARDINESS Frost hardy

FLOWERING Late spring and early summer

Ligularia dentata 'Desdemona' Golden groundsel

L

STRIKING AND IMMENSELY USEFUL, ligularias are suitable for slightly shady, fertile sites where the soil stays moist. If grown in sunnier sites you will have to water copiously in heatwave conditions to prevent the whole plant suddenly collapsing. 'Desdemona' has orange flowers that make a bold statement, appearing on erect stems well above the foliage. Other striking ligularias are available, including the stately 'The Rocket', which can hit 2m (6ft) high. Take precautions against slugs and snails which can be a major nuisance.

OTHER VARIETIES *L. dentata* 'Othello' (deep purplish-green leaves); *L.* 'Gregynog Gold' (taller-growing, golden-orange flowers); *L.* 'The Rocket' (taller-growing, yellow flowers on black stems).

PLANT PROFILE	
HEIGHT 1m (3ft)	
SPREAD 60cm (24in)	
SITE Partial shade	
SOIL Moist, fertile	
HARDINESS Fully hardy	
FLOWERING Midsummer to early autumn	

L | *Ligularia przewalskii*

STRIKING, TALL AND SHOWY, this plant combines three good colours in midsummer: dark green leaves, thin black flower stems, and tall columns of bright yellow tiny flowers. *Ligularia przewalskii* is very effective when planted *en masse* or in small groups dotted through a border, making the eye zigzag from one group of yellow spires to another. There is not much to chose from between this and 'The Rocket', although the leaves of *L. przewalskii* are more dramatically jagged. Moist soil which doesn't dry out in summer is essential – without this, ligularias need copious watering.

OTHER VARIETIES *L. dentata* (smaller-growing, clusters of orange-yellow flowers); *L. hodgsonii* (smaller-growing, yellow-orange flowers).

PLANT PROFILE
HEIGHT To 2m (6ft)
SPREAD 1m (3ft)
SITE Full sun
SOIL Moist, fertile
HARDINESS Frost hardy
FLOWERING Mid- and late summer

Limonium latifolium Sea lavender

L

THE FOAMING MASS OF LAVENDER-BLUE flowers liberally covering the foliage of this plant is an impressive sight. Sea lavender is small enough for most sites and, with its tolerance of salt spray, is typically seen in coastal gardens where it benefits from free-draining soil and bright sun. The flowers of most types of sea lavender are used in displays of cut flowers and for drying. The main problem that affects this plant is powdery mildew, a fungal disease that causes a white, powdery growth on the leaves. It can be kept in check by ensuring the soil is not too dry, or by using proprietary sprays.

OTHER VARIETIES *L. bellidifolium* (smaller-growing, pale violet or blue-violet flowers); *L. platyphyllum* 'Violetta' (deep violet flowers).

PLANT PROFILE
HEIGHT 60cm (24in) or more
SPREAD 45cm (18in)
SITE Full sun
SOIL Free-draining
HARDINESS Fully hardy
FLOWERING Late summer

L

Linaria purpurea 'Canon Went' Toadflax

WITH CLUSTERS OF PALE PINK FLOWERS at the top of tall, thin stems, 'Canon Went' is ideal for cottage gardens, where it adds a free-flowing, open look. Although short-lived, it self-seeds freely and you never have to worry about raising replacements, although if you want to retain the pink colour, you must keep it away from *Linaria purpurea* with which it will cross breed. To keep it in check, remove any unwanted new plants in the spring, and transplant others to a more desirable site. Full sun and good drainage are required.

OTHER VARIETIES *L. dalmatica* (yellow flowers); *L. purpurea* (violet-purple flowers); *L. purpurea* 'Springside White' (white flowers); *L. triornithophora* (purple and yellow flowers with brownish-purple spurs).

PLANT PROFILE

HEIGHT 90cm (36in)

SPREAD 30cm (12in)

SITE Full sun

SOIL Free-draining

HARDINESS Fully hardy

FLOWERING Early summer to early autumn

Linum perenne Perennial flax

L

WITH A CONSTANT SUCCESSION of flowers giving a show of bright blue throughout summer, you don't notice that each flower lasts only a single day. A sunny situation is essential because the blooms tend to stay firmly closed when it's dull and cloudy. A low-growing plant, perennial flax should be placed at the front of a border and planted in light, free-draining soil. The flax is at its best for the first few years, and you should either replace it with cuttings after three years or with one of its seedlings. *Linum narbonense* (flowering flax) is a good alternative – it is slightly bluer, and often lives longer.

OTHER VARIETIES *L. flavum* (smaller-growing, gold flowers); *L.* 'Gemmell's Hybrid' (smaller-growing, chrome-yellow flowers).

PLANT PROFILE
HEIGHT 10–60cm (4–24in)
SPREAD 30cm (12in)
SITE Partial shade
SOIL Free-draining
HARDINESS Fully hardy
FLOWERING Early and midsummer

L *Liriope muscari* Lilyturf

IN CHINA AND JAPAN, lilyturf grows naturally in the acid soil of the woodland floor, and these are the garden conditions it needs – moist but free-draining soil and shelter. The autumn show, with scores of tiny violet-mauve flowers packed around an upright stem, is made even better by the evergreen, strap-shaped leaves. It can be invasive, but if clumps spread too far, slice off the roots with a spade and dig out excess growth. Other good liriopes include 'Monroe White', and 'Variegata' which has creamy-white striped leaves.

OTHER VARIETIES   *L. muscari* 'John Burch' (gold-variegated leaves); *L. muscari* 'Monroe White' (white flowers, needs full shade); *L. spicata* (smaller-growing, violet to white flowers).

PLANT PROFILE

HEIGHT 30cm (12in)

SPREAD 45cm (18in)

SITE Partial or full shade

SOIL Moist but free-draining

HARDINESS Fully hardy

FLOWERING Early to late autumn

Lobelia cardinalis Cardinal flower

L

VIVID SCARLET FLOWERS above dark bronze leaves make this lobelia an essential ingredient for a hot colour scheme. It needs moist soil, however, so if there is any danger of it drying out, add a thick mulch of compost after watering. It is well worth growing a large clump of these plants, partly to make sure lots survive the attention of slugs, and partly because the scarlet flowers makes a striking display. It can also be grown in bog gardens and in shallow water.

OTHER VARIETIES *L. dortmanna* (smaller-growing, blue to pale violet flowers, grows in shallow water); *L.* x *gerardii* 'Vedrariensis' (larger-growing, violet-purple flowers); *L. laxiflora* (yellow flowers, red-tinted stems); *L.* 'Queen Victoria' (scarlet flowers).

PLANT PROFILE
HEIGHT 90cm (36in)
SPREAD 30cm (12in)
SITE Full sun or partial shade
SOIL Moist
HARDINESS Frost hardy
FLOWERING Summer and early autumn

L | *Lunaria rediviva* Perennial honesty

GROWING NATURALLY ON THE EDGES of woodlands, this plant is just right for cottage gardens or for the wilder, outer fringes of a more formal garden design. It has dark green leaves, about 13cm (5in) long or more, with small, delicate, pale lilac-white flowers. The flowers also have a gentle scent. Provide moist, fertile soil for the best results. Like the annual *Lunaria annua*, it produces excellent seedheads that look like silver coins, which is why perennial honesty is sometimes called the money plant. The seedheads can be dried and used in displays for the home.

PLANT PROFILE

HEIGHT 60–90cm (24–36in)

SPREAD 30cm (12in)

SITE Full sun or partial shade

SOIL Moist, fertile

HARDINESS Fully hardy

FLOWERING Late spring and early summer

Lupinus 'My Castle' Lupin

L

ALTHOUGH LUPINS ENCOMPASS annuals and shrubs, this is a clump-forming, soft-red perennial. It mixes well with other lively coloured lupins, and there are plenty available, such as 'Chandelier' (bright yellow), 'The Chatelaine' (pink and white) and 'The Governor' (blue and white). All prefer free-draining soil that is not too rich. New plants can be grown from seed, or take cuttings as soon as the new growth starts. Because lupins are prone to various diseases and are short-lived you will need to replace them every few years.

OTHER VARIETIES *L.* Band of Nobles Series (white, yellow, pink, red, blue, or bicoloured); *L.* 'Noble Maiden' (creamy-white flowers); *L.* 'Thundercloud' (deep violet-blue flowers).

PLANT PROFILE
HEIGHT 90cm (36in)
SPREAD 75cm (30in)
SITE Full sun or partial shade
SOIL Fertile, free-draining
HARDINESS Fully hardy
FLOWERING Early and midsummer

L | *Luzula nivea* Snowy woodrush

THE MOST POPULAR TYPES of woodrush are *Luzula nivea* and the many varieties of *L. sylvatica* (greater woodrush). They are evergreen wild garden or woodland plants that require moist, rich soil and shade. You can grow them out in the open if the soil is mulched with compost and remains damp. *L. nivea* has bright, white flowers above grass-like leaves, while the flowers of *L. sylvatica* make an earlier display, opening in mid-spring. *L. sylvatica* 'Aurea' is an attractive winter performer because of its bright yellow leaves.

OTHER VARIETIES *L. sylvatica* (chestnut-brown flowers); *L. sylvatica* 'Marginata' (pendent, brown and gold flowers, rich green leaves with neat cream margins).

PLANT PROFILE

HEIGHT 60cm (24in)

SPREAD 45cm (18in)

SITE Partial or deep shade

SOIL Moist, fertile

HARDINESS Fully hardy

FLOWERING Early and midsummer

Lychnis chalcedonica Jerusalem cross

L

THE BRIGHT SCARLET FLOWERS of Jerusalem cross immediately grab your attention, and they can be used effectively as a background plant to *Verbena bonariensis*, in knot gardens, and in flashy hot colour schemes. It self-seeds freely and clumps soon form, but they do need some support to prevent their heads from flopping and spoiling the colourful impact. They don't flower beyond midsummer and should be planted next to flowering plants that will keep the show going. The soil needs to be moist, rich, and free-draining.

OTHER VARIETIES *L. coronaria* (shorter, purple-red flowers, silver-grey leaves); *L. coronaria* 'Alba' (white flowers); *L. coronata* var. *sieboldii* (deep red flowers); *L. flos-cuculi* (shorter, bright purplish-pink).

PLANT PROFILE
HEIGHT 1–1.2m (3–4ft)
SPREAD 30cm (12in)
SITE Full sun or partial shade
SOIL Fertile, moist but free-draining
HARDINESS Fully hardy
FLOWERING Early and midsummer

L | *Lychnis coronaria* Rose campion

THIS COTTAGE GARDEN FAVOURITE features strong colour contrasts, making it popular in borders as well. The soft leaves are silver-grey, while the flowers are like flat, purple-red discs. Free-draining soil and constant sun are the keys to success here, and the stems will need staking in exposed, windy gardens to prevent them from flopping. The downy foliage of young plants is visible throughout the winter. Although short-lived, it self-seeds, giving rise to more plants that you can easily fork out and replant to fill any gaps.

OTHER VARIETIES   *L.* x *arkwrightii* 'Vesuvius' (smaller-growing, orange-scarlet flowers, brownish-green leaves); *L. chalcedonica* (taller-growing, scarlet flowers).

PLANT PROFILE	
HEIGHT 80cm (32in)	
SPREAD 45cm (18in)	
SITE Full sun	
SOIL Free-draining	
HARDINESS Fully hardy	
FLOWERING Late summer	

Lysichiton americanus Yellow skunk cabbage

L

GROWING IN THE MUDDY, shallow water of large ponds or streams, the curious flowers of the yellow skunk cabbage produce a flashy touch of bright colour. The flowers are actually attached to the central poker-like growth, and what looks like a giant petal is, in fact, a spathe, or coloured bract (in Greek *Lysichiton* means a loose cloak). Both appear before the large, glossy, veined leaves which, with luck, can grow as long as 1.2m (4ft), so make sure that you provide enough space for them to develop.

OTHER VARIETY *L. camtschatcensis* (green poker and contrasting white spathe, strongly veined dark green leaves).

PLANT PROFILE	
HEIGHT 1m (3ft)	
SPREAD 1.2m (4ft)	
SITE Full sun or partial shade	
SOIL Moist	
HARDINESS Fully hardy	
FLOWERING Early spring	

L

Lysimachia clethroides Loosestrife

ALTHOUGH IT CAN BE INVASIVE, *Lysimachia clethroides* looks best when grown in showy groups. The spires, initially with a crook at the top, have tiny white flowers running up to the tip. Loosestrife needs moist soil and is usually grown either in light shade with a heavy mulch of compost or near natural ponds. A good alternative is the slightly tender, white-flowering *L. epherum*, which tends to bloom more in the first half of summer. Any excess growth can be controlled by digging out unwanted plants.

OTHER VARIETIES *L. ciliata* (taller-growing, yellow flowers with reddish centres); *L. nummularia* 'Aurea' (smaller-growing ground cover, yellow flowers and leaves).

PLANT PROFILE

HEIGHT 90cm (36in)

SPREAD 60cm (24in)

SITE Full sun or partial shade

SOIL Moist

HARDINESS Fully hardy

FLOWERING Mid- and late summer

Lysimachia punctata Loosestrife

L

THIS QUIRKY PLANT sends up stiff, vertical flower stems with short, horizontal leaves ranged up the spire between bright yellow flowers. It is quite invasive, and will soon form a showy colony in the damp soil near a natural pond. You can also grow it in a moist border, although it may intrude on its neighbours, in which case you will have to slice the roots with a spade and dig out any excess growth. A much smaller alternative is the 5cm (2in) high, yellow-leaved *Lysimachia nummularia* 'Aurea' which is also invasive but makes good ground cover.

OTHER VARIETIES *L. clethroides* (white flowers, mid-green leaves); *L. vulgaris* (larger-growing, yellow flowers, bright green leaves).

PLANT PROFILE
HEIGHT 1m (3ft)
SPREAD 60cm (24in)
SITE Full sun or partial shade
SOIL Moist
HARDINESS Fully hardy
FLOWERING Mid- and late summer

L

Lythrum salicaria 'Feuerkerze' Purple loosestrife

NOT TO BE CONFUSED with *Lysimachia*, which is also known as loosestrife and thrives in moist soil, this plant has thin spires covered with rose-red flowers. It makes highly attractive clumps near streams, natural ponds and in bog gardens, but can also be grown in moist borders. A few species of lythrum have become notorious weeds in North America where they spread rapidly but this species, although vigorous, can easily be controlled by digging out the excess growth. Beware of attacks from slugs and snails in the spring.

OTHER VARIETIES *L. salicaria* 'Morden Pink' (clear pink flowers); *L. salicaria* 'Robert' (bright pink flowers); *L. virgatum* 'The Rocket' (smaller-growing, deep pink flowers).

PLANT PROFILE

HEIGHT 90cm (36in)

SPREAD 45cm (18in)

SITE Full sun

SOIL Moist

HARDINESS Fully hardy

FLOWERING Midsummer to early autumn

Macleaya cordata Plume poppy

M

WITH ITS GREY-GREEN STEMS and masses of airy, plume-like flowers, this is an excellent choice for a large border. It needs small plants in front so that its large, shapely, grey to olive-green leaves are not obscured. Plume poppies like rich moist but free-draining soil, although they will tolerate less than ideal conditions and even some shade. Remove excess spreading growth to keep the plant in check. An alternative choice is *Macleaya microcarpa* 'Kelway's Coral Plume' which has coral-pink flowers and is slightly more invasive.

OTHER VARIETIES *M. cordata* 'Flamingo' (buff-pink flowers from pink buds); *M.* x *kewensis* (creamy-buff flowers, grey-green leaves).

PLANT PROFILE
HEIGHT To 2.5m (8ft)
SPREAD 1m (3ft)
SITE Full sun
SOIL Fertile, moist but free-draining
HARDINESS Fully hardy
FLOWERING Mid- and late summer

M | *Maianthemum bifolium* False lily-of-the-valley

PROVIDING GOOD GROUND COVER, false lily-of-the-valley produces a low, quick-spreading mat of glossy leaves. Out of each clump of leaves stems carrying four-petalled flowers appear in the spring (in mild weather) or early summer, and these are followed by small, bright red berries. Due to its invasive nature, this is definitely not a plant for the border; instead, grow it in wild or woodland gardens where it can multiply freely. The soil should be rich and moist, without being boggy, and neutral to slightly acid.

PLANT PROFILE

HEIGHT 15cm (6in)

SPREAD Indefinite

SITE Light dappled or deep shade

SOIL Fertile, moist but free-draining

HARDINESS Fully hardy

FLOWERING Early summer

Malva moschata f. *alba* Musk mallow

M

AVAILABLE IN SHADES OF WHITE, PINK, blue, and purple, mallows are frustratingly short-lived, although they do self-seed. This form of the plant has gently scented white flowers that gradually take on a pink tinge, and is a good contender for a cottage garden. It is bushy and stands up straight, and can be planted alongside the pink-flowered *Malva moschata*. Both need free-draining soil and some support when grown on exposed, windy sites. If they are being grown on heavy clay soil, treat them as annuals – collect seed in the autumn and grow new plants each year.

OTHER VARIETIES *M. alcea* var. *fastigiata* (smaller-growing, deep pink flowers); *M. sylvestris* (veined pinkish-purple flowers).

PLANT PROFILE

HEIGHT 90cm (36in)

SPREAD 60cm (24in)

SITE Full sun

SOIL Free-draining

HARDINESS Fully hardy

FLOWERING Early summer to early autumn

M | *Meconopsis betonicifolia* Himalayan blue poppy

THE TIBETAN BLUE POPPY, as it is also known, is an absolute delight. It has open, clear blue flowers with four petals and an inner eye of yellow anthers. It needs a cool climate and soil that never dries out, remaining moist all summer. If you have suitable conditions for this poppy, plant it in drifts or small groups in a border. If conditions are less than favourable, it will flower in its first summer and then die, but even as an annual it's definitely worth growing. You can raise it from seed, but it's easier to buy new young plants.

OTHER VARIETIES *M. grandis* (rich blue to purplish-red flowers); *M. napaulensis* (larger-growing, pink, red, or purple flowers).

PLANT PROFILE	
HEIGHT	1.2m (4ft)
SPREAD	45cm (18in)
SITE	Partial shade
SOIL	Moist
HARDINESS	Fully hardy
FLOWERING	Early summer

Meconopsis cambrica Welsh poppy

M

GROWING WILD IN WALES in shady areas where the soil is moist, the Welsh poppy will, with luck, self-seed around the garden. If you find seedlings popping up in open, hot, dry areas, move them immediately so that their roots are in moist, cool soil. Welsh poppies represent excellent value, flowering throughout the summer months, and even a single plant, if it is strategically placed, can be a real gem. Use it in a shady spot in a wildflower garden or to brighten up a bed beneath trees or shrubs.

OTHER VARIETIES *M. quintuplinervia* (pale lavender-blue or purplish-blue flowers); *M.* x *sheldonii* (larger-growing, deep rich to pale blue flowers).

PLANT PROFILE
HEIGHT 45cm (18in)
SPREAD 25cm (10in)
SITE Partial shade
SOIL Moist
HARDINESS Fully hardy
FLOWERING Mid-spring to mid-autumn

M | *Melianthus major* Honey bush

A MUST FOR GARDENS featuring architectural plants, *Melianthus major* has beautiful, shapely leaves, each up to 50cm (20in) long. Technically a shrub, it performs like a perennial in cold-climate gardens because the top-growth dies back in winter; even if it does not die, it should be pruned to the ground in spring. Later, superb, fresh, multi-fingered leaves open before the insignificant flowers appear. Plants need a sheltered, sunny position on moist but free-draining, fertile ground. Provide a thick winter mulch of compost to protect the young roots, and although mature plants should survive bad winters, keep on mulching. It makes a good combination when positioned behind eryngiums (sea holly) – both have shapely foliage, with that of the latter being smaller and spiky.

PLANT PROFILE

HEIGHT	2–3m (6–10ft)
SPREAD	1–3m (3–10ft)
SITE	Full sun
SOIL	Fertile, moist but free-draining
HARDINESS	Half hardy
FLOWERING	Late spring to midsummer

Melica altissima 'Atropurpurea' Siberian melick

M

NATIVE TO CENTRAL AND EASTERN EUROPE, this decorative grass grows in shrubby thickets and at the edges of forests. It makes an upright clump with purple-mauve flower spikes that gradually fade in colour as they age. 'Atropurpurea' grows equally well in light shade or hot, sunny sites, and the foliage can be left to stand over winter, adding shape and interest to the garden – then cut it away in spring before the new growth begins. 'Alba' has white flower spikes, and both forms are useful in cut-flower displays.

OTHER VARIETIES *M. nutans* (smaller-growing, brown and cream flower spikes from late spring, fresh green leaves); *M. uniflora* 'Variegata' (smaller-growing, fresh green leaves with creamy stripes).

PLANT PROFILE	
HEIGHT To 1.5m (5ft)	
SPREAD To 80cm (32in)	
SITE Full sun or light shade	
SOIL Moist, free-draining	
HARDINESS Fully hardy	
FLOWERING Summer	

M | *Melissa officinalis* 'Aurea' Lemon balm

FOR MEDITERRANEAN-STYLE or herb gardens, pots or borders, this plant is perfect. It is widely grown for its lemon-scented, yellow-splashed leaves, although the colour tends to fade in summer. The flowers are pale and small, and should be cut off once they start to fade to prevent self-seeding. Lemon balm needs light, free-draining soil that is quite poor; if it sits in cold, wet soil it will rot. When using the leaves for a pot-pourri or cooking, they are at their most highly scented as the flowers start to open in early summer.

OTHER VARIETIES *M. officinalis* (pale yellow flowers, light green leaves); *M. officinalis* 'All Gold' (white flowers, yellow leaves).

PLANT PROFILE

HEIGHT 60–120cm (24–48in)

SPREAD 30–45cm (12–18in)

SITE Full sun

SOIL Poor, free-draining

HARDINESS Fully hardy

FLOWERING Summer

Melittis melissophyllum Bastard balm

M

IN THE WILD, this plant grows in patchy woodland in Europe. It is related to dead nettles and has unusual, spotted flowers, about 4cm (1½in) long, with pink or purple lips. The flowers appear in clusters of two to six, and act as a magnet to bees, while the leaves have the gentle scent of honey. If you cannot reproduce a woodland-type setting in your garden, then use *Melittis melissophyllum* at the front of a border, but you must provide partial shade and moist, free-draining soil that never becomes too dry. Propagate plants by division in the spring, just as the new growth gets under way.

PLANT PROFILE	
HEIGHT 20–70cm (8–28in)	
SPREAD 50cm (20in)	
SITE Partial shade	
SOIL Moist, free-draining	
HARDINESS Fully hardy	
FLOWERING Late spring and early summer	

M | *Mentha suaveolens* 'Variegata' Pineapple mint

THIS IS A STRIKING VARIEGATED plant, with soft hairy leaves with the scent of pineapple. The eye-catching foliage and the fact that it is not rampantly invasive make it a good choice for herb gardens. Like most mints, its spread can be controlled by planting it in a sunken, bottomless bucket filled with moist, infertile soil. Sections can be snipped off and planted in large pots to bring indoors over winter, when the leaves can be used to flavour peas, beans, lamb, and fish, as well as home-made lemonade.

OTHER VARIETIES *M. aquatica* (smaller-growing maginal aquatic, lilac flowers, aromatic dark green leaves); *M. longifolia* (taller-growing, lilac or white flowers, musty scented silver-grey leaves).

PLANT PROFILE

HEIGHT To 1m (3ft)

SPREAD Indefinite

SITE Full sun

SOIL Moist

HARDINESS Fully hardy

FLOWERING Summer

Milium effusum 'Aureum' Bowles' golden grass

M

IN THE SPRING when the young, strap-shaped foliage is a bright, vivid, yellowish-green, this perennial looks extremely smart. It makes an even better show in light shade – its preferred site – adding much-needed colour to these areas. By midsummer the leaves have lost much of their fresh colour and turn slightly green. 'Aureum' rarely lives for long, but it is a modest self-seeder and should provide a steady supply of replacements. The soil needs to be moist and rich. If 'Aureum' is being grown in a more open, sunnier position, apply a thick mulch of compost to lock moisture in the ground.

OTHER VARIETY *M. effusum* 'Yaffle' (taller-growing, golden leaves with a pale green stripe).

PLANT PROFILE
HEIGHT To 60cm (24in)
SPREAD 30cm (12in)
SITE Partial shade
SOIL Moist, fertile
HARDINESS Fully hardy
FLOWERING Late spring to midsummer

GRASS SEEDS

Fully fluffed-up grass heads, or inflorescences (above), are full of seeds. If you cut the stems too soon (top), the head will contain unripe seed.

M | *Miscanthus sinensis* 'Silberfeder'

SOME OF THE BEST flowering grasses available for gardens are found in this group of plants, and at 2.5m (8ft) 'Silberfeder' is one of the tallest. The large clump of foliage is topped by beautiful plumes of feathery flowerheads, held up high to catch the breeze. The thin, strap-like leaves are on the lax side, and tend to arch over and flop, which gives 'Silberfeder' a rather graceful look. The grasses grow in most gardens, enjoying decent drainage and average fertility.

OTHER VARIETIES *M. sinensis* 'Rotsilber' (smaller-growing, red-tinted silver heads); *M. sinensis* 'Zebrinus' (smaller-growing, arching leaves with creamy-white or pale yellow horizontal bands).

PLANT PROFILE

HEIGHT 2.5m (8ft)

SPREAD 1.2m (4ft)

SITE Full sun

SOIL Average, free-draining

HARDINESS Fully hardy

FLOWERING Autumn

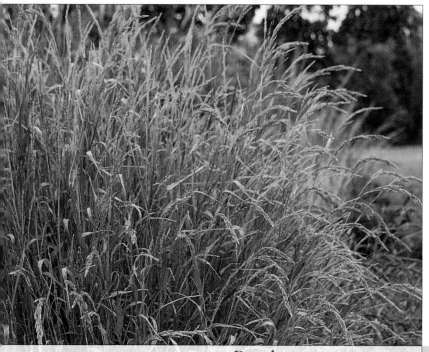

Molinia caerulea subsp. *caerulea* 'Moorhexe' Purple moor grass

M

MOST OF THE MOLINIAS are tall grasses, up to 2.2m (7ft) high, but this is an extremely useful small moor grass. Smartly upright with green leaves, it needs a position right at the front of a border or you could plant it in groups around the feet of a pergola. For a much bigger plant go for a form of *Molinia caerulea* subsp. *arundinacea*, such as the tall, very upright 'Sky Racer'. All moor grasses have rich, yellow-orange tints in the autumn, and should be grown in moist but free-draining, acid to neutral soil.

OTHER VARIETIES *M. caerulea* subsp. *arundinacea* 'Karl Foerster' (larger-growing, purple flowerheads on arching stems); *M. caerulea* subsp. *caerulea* 'Variegata' (cream-striped leaves, ochre stems).

PLANT PROFILE		
HEIGHT 45cm (18in)		
SPREAD 40cm (16in)		
SITE Full sun or partial shade		
SOIL Moist but free-draining		
HARDINESS Fully hardy		
FLOWERING Spring to autumn		

M | *Moltkia doerfleri*

WITH ITS SPECIFIC CULTIVATION REQUIREMENTS, which include very free-draining soil with average to poor fertility, *Moltkia doerfleri* is a perfect plant for the top of a dry-stone wall, or a rock or gravel garden. Its stiff, wiry, erect stems are covered in deep purple flowers in the first part of summer, often starting in late spring, and the leaves are mid-green, narrowly lance-shaped, and about 5cm (2in) long. Although hardy, it dislikes being exposed to icy winds and standing in wet soil, preferring a sheltered, warm position. Other types tend to be shrubby with blue, purple, or yellow flowers.

PLANT PROFILE

HEIGHT 30–50cm (12–20in)

SPREAD 30–50cm (12–20in)

SITE Full sun

SOIL Poor, free-draining

HARDINESS Fully hardy

FLOWERING Late spring to midsummer

Monarda 'Cambridge Scarlet' Bergamot

M

THE MIDSUMMER FLOWERS of this plant are a combination of rich red and scarlet and look best when grown in groups in a border. They make a striking show, but are likely to upstage any nearby pastel colours. Many monardas have leaves with a strong citrus scent suitable for pot-pourri. Moist, rich soil is the key to success in summer, but you must avoid wet ground in winter. Mulch plants well to lock in soil moisture and to help prevent powdery mildew which can be a major problem during long hot spells.

OTHER VARIETIES *M.* 'Beauty of Cobham' (pink flowers, purple bracts); *M.* 'Croftway Pink' (rose-pink flowers and bracts); *M. didyma* (pink flowers, red bracts); *M.* 'Vintage Wine' (reddish flowers, brown bracts).

PLANT PROFILE

HEIGHT 90cm (36in)

SPREAD 45cm (18in)

SITE Full sun or dappled shade

SOIL Fertile, moist but free-draining

HARDINESS Fully hardy

FLOWERING Midsummer to early autumn

M Morina longifolia Whorlflower

A ROSETTE OF SHINY, spiny evergreen leaves, each up to 30cm (12in) long, appears on the ground, giving this plant an intriguing, striking look. From the rosette a vertical flowering stem shoots up. The white flowers grow in whorls or tiers up the stem, and the blooms are held in green bracts. It is fussy in its requirements and to ensure success the crown needs winter protection with a mulch of bracken to protect it from wind and frost, while the roots demand free-draining soil that never bakes dry. Before planting, dig well-rotted compost into the soil to improve its structure.

PLANT PROFILE

HEIGHT 90cm (36in) or more

SPREAD 50cm (20in)

SITE Full sun

SOIL Free-draining

HARDINESS Fully hardy

FLOWERING Midsummer

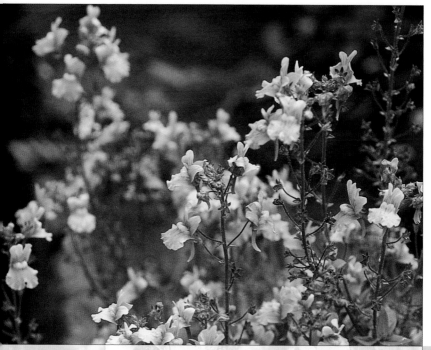

Nemesia denticulata

N

IN ITS NATIVE SOUTHERN AFRICA, this plant grows in sandy, rocky sites, and produces flowers mainly in pink, mauve, and white. In the garden, the small, scented flowers need to be placed at the front of a display or they can be overlooked. It may survive winter in cold-climate gardens, but to be safe grow it in a warm, sheltered position with very good drainage – at the base of a sunny wall, for example – or pot it up in the autumn and keep it in a frost-free greenhouse until the following spring. If growing it outdoors, cut the stems back in spring once frosts are over, and water well during dry spells.

OTHER VARIETIES *N. caerulea* (taller-growing, pink, pale blue, lavender-blue, or white flowers); *N.* 'Innocence' (white flowers).

PLANT PROFILE
HEIGHT 25cm (10in)
SPREAD 30cm (12in)
SITE Full sun
SOIL Moist, free-draining
HARDINESS Frost hardy
FLOWERING Summer to early autumn

N | *Nepeta sibirica* Catmint

IF YOU WANT TO DRIVE CATS WILD and attract bees to your garden, this is the plant for you. It has strongly scented, dark grey leaves and a haze of light blue flowers. Shorter catmints, such as *Nepeta racemosa*, are best planted at the front of a border or edging a path, but this tall variety can be placed further back. The soil should be free-draining and on the dry side, although some types, such as *N. subsessilis*, are suitable for shady, moist gardens.

OTHER VARIETIES *N. govaniana* (yellow flowers, shady, moist sites); *N. sibirica* 'Souvenir d'André Chaudron' (smaller-growing, dark lavender-blue flowers, grey-green leaves); *N.* 'Six Hills Giant' (lavender-blue flowers, grey-green leaves); *N. subsessilis* (bright blue flowers, shady, moist sites).

PLANT PROFILE
HEIGHT 90cm (36in)
SPREAD 45cm (18in)
SITE Full sun or partial shade
SOIL Free-draining
HARDINESS Fully hardy
FLOWERING Mid- and late summer

Nicotiana sylvestris Tobacco plant

N

TALL, UPRIGHT, AND SCENTED, this tall tobacco plant makes a classy ingredient for a cottage garden, as well as for more formal designs. The stems shoot up from large, ground-hugging leaves, which can reach a length of 35cm (14in), and hold long, thin, tubular, white flowers with a rich, sweet scent. Plant *Nicotiana sylvestris* in clumps, or circles around a feature plant, in rich, free-draining soil. It is short-lived and won't survive the winter outside, but is easy to grow from seed collected in the autumn. Leave space for the large leaves or they will obscure smaller, neighbouring plants as they grow.

OTHER VARIETIES *N. alata* (greenish-yellow flowers, white within); *N. x sanderae* (red, rose-pink, purple, or sometimes white flowers).

PLANT PROFILE
HEIGHT To 1.5m (5ft)
SPREAD To 60cm (24in)
SITE Full sun or partial shade
SOIL Fertile, free-draining
HARDINESS Half hardy
FLOWERING Summer

O *Oenanthe javanica* 'Flamingo'

GROWING IN BOG GARDENS or water meadows, or close to natural ponds or streams, the moisture-loving 'Flamingo' produces attractive pink, cream, and white foliage. The tiny, star-shaped white flowers appear in small sprays in the second half of summer and, with the clusters of multicoloured leaves on long stalks, make useful components in cut-flower displays. Don't be put off by some reports that 'Flamingo' is highly toxic – it is safe, and is even eaten as a vegetable in some regions of the world (from India to Japan). Other types of *Oenanthe*, however, are toxic.

PLANT PROFILE
HEIGHT 20–40cm (8–16in)
SPREAD 90cm (36in)
SITE Full sun or partial shade
SOIL Moist
HARDINESS Frost hardy
FLOWERING Late summer

Oenothera fruticosa 'Fyrverkeri' Evening primrose

O

JAZZING UP THE SUMMER GARDEN, the flowers of this plant are startling bright yellow, shaped like saucers and arranged right the way up short, red-tinged stems. 'Fyrverkeri', which is also known as 'Fireworks', scores even more points because its young leaves have a reddish-purple tinge, making a lively contrast with the stems. It needs to be positioned with care, and kept away from plants with more subdued colours as these will be pushed into the background once the flowers open. The key to success with evening primrose is sandy, free-draining soil.

OTHER VARIETIES *O. fruticosa* subsp. *glauca* (light yellow flowers); *O. fruticosa* subsp. *glauca* 'Erica Robin' (young red foliage, golden flowers).

PLANT PROFILE
HEIGHT 30–100cm (12–39in)
SPREAD 30cm (12in)
SITE Full sun
SOIL Free-draining
HARDINESS Fully hardy
FLOWERING Late spring to late summer

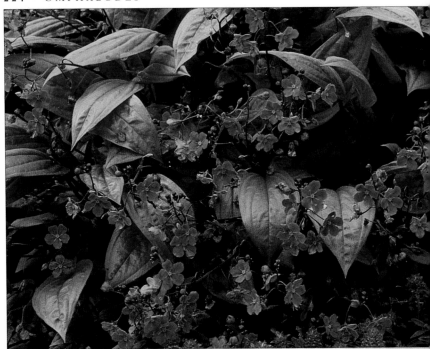

O

Omphalodes cappadocica 'Cherry Ingram' Navelwort

THE LARGE, DARK BLUE FLOWERS with white centres make 'Cherry Ingram' a better choice than the parent plant, *Omphalodes cappadocica*, which has smaller, lighter flowers. This is a pretty plant for a wild garden or for growing among shrubs in the border, adding sprays of blue in the early spring. It is particularly valuable because it tolerates a shady garden position, and where grown on moist, rich soil, will make attractive clumps. Navelwort mixes well with primulas that like the same site and soil conditions. A good alternative is 'Starry Eyes' which has a white stripe on each petal.

OTHER VARIETIES *O. cappadocica* 'Lilac Mist' (lilac-blue flowers); *O. verna* (blue, smaller flowers).

PLANT PROFILE	
HEIGHT To 25cm (10in)	
SPREAD To 40cm (16in)	
SITE Partial shade	
SOIL Moist, fertile	
HARDINESS Fully hardy	
FLOWERING Early spring	

Ophiopogon planiscapus 'Nigrescens' Lilyturf

O

APPEARANCES CAN BE DECEPTIVE. Although this plant looks like a miniature, black-leaved grass with outward-radiating, splayed leaves, it is, in fact, an evergreen perennial. Highly fashionable, 'Nigrescens' is often used to set off larger, more dominant architectural plants, such as cordylines or yuccas. The black leaves stand out well against pale gravel, and it requires slightly acid, free-draining, fertile soil. *Ophiopogon jaburan* 'Vittatus' is another worthwhile, although not totally hardy lilyturf, with green- and cream-striped leaves.

OTHER VARIETIES *O. japonicus* (taller-growing, white, bell-shaped flowers, dark green leaves, blue-black berries); *O. planiscapus* (pale purplish-white flowers, dark green leaves, blue-black berries)

PLANT PROFILE
HEIGHT 20cm (8in)
SPREAD 30cm (12in)
SITE Full sun or light shade
SOIL Acid, fertile, free-draining
HARDINESS Fully hardy
FLOWERING Summer

O   *Osteospermum jucundum*

LARGE, BRIGHT, DAISY-LIKE FLOWERS are the chief characteristic of osteospermums, some, such as 'Whirligig", with petals like outward-radiating spokes with a tiny bulge at the end. They need plenty of sun and free-draining soil, and most won't survive cold, wet winters. This is one of the hardiest, however, and throughout the summer it produces mauve-pink flowers with a yellow eye. It makes a good-size clump for the front of a border or softening the edges of a path.

OTHER VARIETIES *O.* 'Buttermilk' (larger-growing, primrose-yellow flowers with a bluish-mauve eye); *O.* 'Cannington Roy' (smaller-growing, purple-tipped white flowers with a purple eye); *O. ecklonis* (larger-growing, white flowers, indigo blue on the reverse, with a dark blue eye).

PLANT PROFILE
HEIGHT 25cm (10in)
SPREAD 50–90cm (20–36in)
SITE Full sun
SOIL Free-draining
HARDINESS Fully hardy
FLOWERING Late spring to autumn

Oxalis 'Ione Hecker' Shamrock

O

THE DIMINUTIVE SIZE of this perennial demands a place in a rock garden, raised bed or trough. The flowers have five petals with thin, dark purple veins, and it has small, ornamental leaves. Other equally pretty types are available, such as the purple-pink *Oxalis adenophylla*, the yellow *O. lobata*, and *O. versicolor* which has white flowers with crimson margins on the underside. These oxalis like free-draining soil, and although 'Ione Hecker' is hardy, the others are not and need a sunny, sheltered position to survive in cold-climate gardens.

OTHER VARIETIES *O. depressa* (rose-pink to purple-pink flowers); *O. enneaphylla* 'Minutifolia' (compact with white flowers); *O. laciniata* (fragrant, lilac-blue, red, pink, or white flowers).

PLANT PROFILE	
HEIGHT 8cm (3in)	
SPREAD 10cm (4in)	
SITE Full or partial shade	
SOIL Free-draining	
HARDINESS Fully hardy	
FLOWERING Summer	

Pachyphragma macrophyllum

FOR LIGHT SHADE AND MOIST, leafy soil, this plant is a real garden asset. It flowers before the leaves have fully developed and provides sprays of fresh, white petals. Although not exactly invasive, it does provide good cover underneath trees and deciduous shrubs, where it creeps and spreads across the soil. After the vivid show of flowers has finished, semi-evergreen, glossy, dark green leaves fill out and help to suppress any emerging weeds. It may be tempting to cut the flowers for use in an indoor display, but it is worth noting that they do have a slightly unpleasant smell close up.

PLANT PROFILE
HEIGHT 20–40cm (8–16in)
SPREAD 60–90cm (24–36in)
SITE Partial shade
SOIL Moist
HARDINESS Fully hardy
FLOWERING Early spring

Pachysandra terminalis

P

THIS EVERGREEN PLANT IS SUITABLE for even the densest shade in the garden. Its stems spread vigorously, rooting as they go, to make carpets of shiny green foliage. The leaves grow almost in rosettes and are about 10cm (4in) long, pointing outward. Short flower spikes appear in the spring, with tiny white flowers opening at the end of the season or in early summer. *Pachysandra terminalis* needs moist soil with plenty of leaf mould incorporated into it; this plant will not succeed in dry shade. A good, slightly less vigorous alternative is *P. terminalis* 'Variegata' which has attractive creamy-white markings on the edges of its leaves.

OTHER VARIETY *P. terminalis* 'Green Carpet' (finely toothed leaves).

PLANT PROFILE

HEIGHT 20cm (8in)

SPREAD Indefinite

SITE Full or partial shade

SOIL Moist

HARDINESS Fully hardy

FLOWERING Late spring

P

Paeonia lactiflora 'Sarah Bernhardt'

THE SUMPTUOUS FLOWERS of peonies provide some of the best garden displays. There is a wide choice of colours, mainly white, yellow, red, and pink, and the flowers often have a spicy scent. 'Sarah Bernhardt' is scented, soft pink with frilly petals. If space allows, also grow the pink 'Bowl of Beauty', white 'Félix Crousse', and yellow *Paeonia mlokosewitschii*. All should be more to the front than the middle of a border so that they can be fully appreciated. Provide rich, moist but free-draining soil, and support for the stems. Once in the ground and established, they don't like to be disturbed.

OTHER VARIETIES *P. cambessedesii* (smaller-growing, single, deep pink flowers); *P. lactiflora* (single, fragrant, white to pale pink flowers).

PLANT PROFILE	
HEIGHT 90cm (36in)	
SPREAD 90cm (36in)	
SITE Full sun or partial shade	
SOIL Fertile, moist but free-draining	
HARDINESS Fully hardy	
FLOWERING Summer	

Panicum virgatum 'Heavy Metal' Blue switch grass

P

NATIVE TO THE AMERICAN PRAIRIES, there are several outstanding types of *Panicum virgatum*. 'Heavy Metal' is graceful with almost vertical, strappy leaves, about 60cm (24in) high, that are tinged blue and turn yellow in the autumn. Light, airy flowers crest the top of the leaves. 'Prairie Sky' is slightly bluer but tends to flop after a heavy downpour, while 'Hänse Herms' (red switch grass) becomes progressively reddish over summer. Switch grass grows well in most gardens, but won't tolerate either wet or dry extremes. Also, choose the planting position with care and, if possible, site it where the flowers will stand out against a dark background.

OTHER VARIETY *P. virgatum* 'Rehbraun' (burgundy-red foliage).

PLANT PROFILE	
HEIGHT 1.2m (4ft)	
SPREAD 75cm (30in)	
SITE Full sun	
SOIL Moist but free-draininng	
HARDINESS Fully hardy	
FLOWERING Early autumn	

Use a trowel to carefully lift self-sown seedlings, each with its own root ball, from around the parent plant, and replant in any convenient gaps.

P

Papaver orientale 'Mrs. Perry' Oriental poppy

FORMING SMALL, SUBSTANTIAL CLUMPS, these poppies have hairy stems, leaves up to 30cm (12in) long, and buds that start to appear in late spring. These grow larger and larger until the flowers pop out and, at 15cm (6in) across, they really grab the eye. 'Mrs. Perry' is a soft salmon-pink, but there are louder colours, such as the bright red 'Beauty of Livermere' with a black blotch like a huge bumble bee hiding in the base of the flower. Each flower lasts about three days, but more open in succession.

OTHER VARIETIES *P. orientale* 'Allegro' (orange-scarlet flowers); *P. orientale* 'Perry's White' (white flowers with maroon-purple flowers); *P. orientale* 'Picotée' (white flowers with frilly orange-pink margins).

PLANT PROFILE

HEIGHT 45–90cm (18–36in)

SPREAD 60–90cm (24–36in)

SITE Full sun

SOIL Fertile, free-draining

HARDINESS Fully hardy

FLOWERING Late spring to midsummer

Paradisea liliastrum Paradise lily

P

NOT AS POPULAR TODAY as it once was, *Paradisea liliastrum* imparts a lily-like touch to the garden when its trumpet-shaped, scented, white flowers open above grassy leaves in late spring. Not very tall, it is best given a position toward the front of a border or near shrubs, and needs to be planted in rich, moist but free-draining soil. The paradise lily can be difficult to find, but once it's established in the garden it should develop into a good-sized clump. Divide it in autumn to provide extra plants, and keep an eye out for attacks from slugs and snails.

OTHER VARIETY *P. lusitanica* (larger-growing, white flowers).

PLANT PROFILE
HEIGHT 30–60cm (12–24in)
SPREAD 30cm (12in)
SITE Sun or light shade
SOIL Moist, fertile, free-draining
HARDINESS Fully hardy
FLOWERING Late spring or early summer

P | *Parahebe perfoliata* Digger's speedwell

THIS SPREADING EVERGREEN from Australia has floppy, wiry stems, with blue-green leaves and violet-blue flowers. It thrives in poor soil with good drainage, and can be grown in soil-filled cracks in walls, rock or gravel gardens, or near the front of a border. There are several good alternatives, including the shrubby *Parahebe cataractae* 'Delight' with red-veined violet-blue flowers. They all combine well, but digger's speedwell is one of the tallest. Avoid a position where it is exposed to cold, drying winds.

OTHER VARIETIES *P.* x *bidwillii* 'Kea' (smaller-growing, crimson-veined white flowers); *P. cataractae* (smaller-growing, purple-veined white flowers); *P. lyallii* (smaller-growing, blue flowers).

PLANT PROFILE

HEIGHT 60–75cm (24–30in)

SPREAD 45cm (18in)

SITE Full sun

SOIL Poor, free-draining

HARDINESS Frost hardy

FLOWERING Late summer

Pennisetum orientale Oriental fountain grass

P

DISTINCTIVE BOTTLEBRUSH-LIKE FLOWERS emerging from beautiful, arching foliage on top of long, thin stems are the key features of this plant. From a distance the flowers look as if they are covered in tiny pieces of cotton wool and add a soft touch to a gravel garden or a border. It is slightly tender and needs a warm, sheltered site, and soil with very good drainage. Leave the stems standing over winter to add shape and structure to the garden at this time of year, and cut them back in early spring before the new growth begins.

OTHER VARIETIES *P. alopecuroides* 'Hameln' (larger-growing, greenish-white flowers, golden-yellow autumn leaves); *P. macrourum* (smaller-growing, pale green, bristly flowers).

PLANT PROFILE
HEIGHT 60cm (24in)
SPREAD 75cm (30in)
SITE Full sun
SOIL Free-draining
HARDINESS Frost hardy
FLOWERING Mid- and late summer

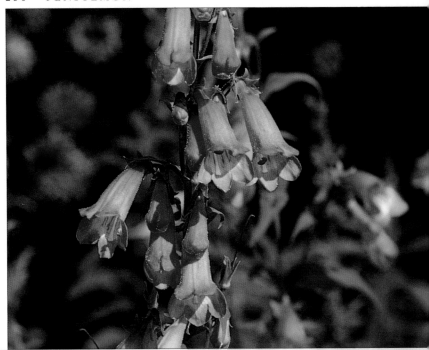

P

Penstemon 'Pennington Gem'

PROLIFIC AND EASY TO GROW, penstemons perform throughout the summer and are terrific garden value. They come in white, purple, red, pink, mauve, blue, and even yellow, most with a white throat. 'Pennington Gem' has typical, downward-pointing tubular flowers held on stiff, upright stems, and can be used virtually anywhere in the border. It is only frost hardy, however, and needs a warm, sunny garden position, and free-draining, fertile soil. Cuttings taken in summer quickly root and guarantee plants for the following year.

OTHER VARIETIES *P.* 'Alice Hindley' (larger-growing, lilac-blue flowers); *P.* 'Apple Blossom' (smaller-growing, pale pink flowers); *P.* 'Sour Grapes' (smaller-growing, greyish-blue flowers).

PLANT PROFILE
HEIGHT 75cm (30in)
SPREAD 45cm (18in)
SITE Full sun
SOIL Fertile, free-draining
HARDINESS Frost hardy
FLOWERING Midsummer to mid-autumn

Pentaglottis sempervirens Green alkanet

P

THINK CAREFULLY about installing this plant, because once it is in your garden it can be extremely difficult to eradicate. It self-seeds, and if any slivers of its deep root are left when you are attempting to dig it out, they will regrow. Nonetheless, it makes very effective ground cover for a shady site, and has leaves up to 40cm (16in) long and bright blue flowers like those of a forget-me-not (*Myosotis*). The best place for green alkanet is a wild or woodland garden, where the soil is moist and rich and it can spread at will. To prevent the plant self-seeding, shear it over as soon as the flowers start to fade.

PLANT PROFILE
HEIGHT 70–100cm (28–39in)
SPREAD 70–100cm (28–39in)
SITE Partial or deep shade
SOIL Moist, fertile
HARDINESS Fully hardy
FLOWERING Spring to early summer

P

Persicaria affinis 'Donald Lowndes' Knotweed

KNOTWEED IS A LOW-KEY PLANT, great for filling gaps in a border or providing ground cover. More suitable for a border, 'Donald Lowndes' is distinguished by short spikes of pale pink flowers, held up like candles above the leaves. It needs moist soil, but if you have free-draining conditions, try *Persicaria bisorta* instead. Other good varieties include 'Darjeeling Red' which initially has pink flowers that darken to red, and 'Superba' with its deep pinkish-red blooms that become redder as the summer progresses.

OTHER VARIETIES *P. amplexicaulis* (taller, bright red to purple or white flowers); *P. bistorta* 'Superba' (taller, soft pink flowers); *P. campanulata* (taller, fragrant, pink or white flowers); *P. milletii* (taller, crimson flowers).

PLANT PROFILE

HEIGHT 20cm (8in)

SPREAD 30cm (12in)

SITE Full sun or partial shade

SOIL Moist

HARDINESS Fully hardy

FLOWERING Midsummer to mid-autumn

Phalaris arundinacea var. *picta* 'Picta' Gardener's garters

P

SOMETIMES KNOWN AS RIBBON GRASS, if this plant is allowed the space to roam in a wild garden, near a natural pond, or even right up to the water's edge, it makes a wonderful sight – especially in late spring and early summer. It needs to be planted with care, however, because in rich, moist soil it can be very invasive. The evergreen foliage has fresh green and white stripes, and it should be sheared over after flowering to provide a second flush of leaves. This also prevents the plants from reverting to all-green foliage.

OTHER VARIETY *P. arundinacea* var. *picta* 'Feesey' (purplish blue flowers, light green leaves with white stripes, stem bases flushed pink).

PLANT PROFILE
HEIGHT 1m (3ft)
SPREAD Indefinite
SITE Full sun or partial shade
SOIL Moist
HARDINESS Fully hardy
FLOWERING Early and midsummer

P

Phlomis russeliana

INTERESTING AND UNUSUAL-LOOKING, this perennial has circular clusters of hooded, pale yellow flowers spaced out at intervals up its vertical stems. Although it doesn't make a powerful colour statement in the garden, it adds a quirky surprise. It grows in most situations, provided it has average, free-draining soil and, like most phlomis, it is just about drought-tolerant. This makes it an ideal candidate for a gravel garden or a dry, sunny border. The seedheads add an extra dimension of interest in winter.

OTHER VARIETY *P. bovei* subsp. *maroccana* (larger-growing, purple-pink flowers with purple spots inside the petals, white-woolly outside, grey-green leaves).

PLANT PROFILE

HEIGHT To 1m (3ft)

SPREAD 75cm (30in)

SITE Full sun or light shade

SOIL Average, free-draining

HARDINESS Fully hardy

FLOWERING Late spring to early autumn

With all phlox species, as soon as the blooms start to fade, cut back the spent flower stems. This will tidy up the plant and encourage more flowering sideshoots to develop.

Phlox paniculata 'Starfire' Perennial phlox

P

THESE SHOWY BORDER PLANTS have an eye-catching domed head of flowers in a wide range of colours. They are best grown in sizeable groups to provide wafting sweet scent in the early evening. Use the same colours together or the effect can become spotty. 'Starfire' is at the hot-hued end of the spectrum, and contrasts well with 'White Admiral' or 'Blue Boy'. Good pastels include pale lilac 'Prospero' and pale pink 'Sandringham'. Average garden soil is fine, with well-rotted compost forked in. For extra flowers, deadhead throughout summer.

OTHER VARIETIES *P. paniculata* 'Brigadier' (pinkish–red flowers); *P. paniculata* 'Fujiyama' (white flowers); *P. paniculata* 'Le Mahdi' (bluish–purple flowers); *P. paniculata* 'Windsor' (reddish–pink flowers).

PLANT PROFILE
HEIGHT 90cm (36in)
SPREAD 45cm (18in)
SITE Full sun or partial shade
SOIL Average, free-draining
HARDINESS Fully hardy
FLOWERING Summer to early or mid-autumn

P

Phormium tenax New Zealand flax

THE SWORD-LIKE, EVERGREEN LEAVES of this striking plant are up to 3m (10ft) high, while the summer flower spikes, bearing dull red flowers, tower above them. Use it as a focal feature in a gravel or Mediterranean-style garden, or in a large pot. Since this flax is not totally hardy add a thick mulch or layer of bracken around the base of the plant for winter or, if growing in a pot, move it to a warm spot. Divide plants every three years, keeping an outer section with leaves and roots – established plants may be impossible to dig up.

OTHER VARIETIES *P. cookianum* subsp. *hookeri* 'Tricolor' (smaller, yellow-green flowers, leaves with cream and red margins); *P.* 'Sundowner' (smaller, bronze-green leaves with pink margins).

PLANT PROFILE

HEIGHT 4m (12ft)

SPREAD 2m (6ft)

SITE Full sun

SOIL Fertile, free-draining

HARDINESS Frost hardy

FLOWERING Summer

Phragmites australis subsp. *australis* 'Variegatus' Common reed

IF YOU HAVE A BOG GARDEN, very large pond or streamside bank you can take on this invasive perennial. It can stand in water up to 1.5m (5ft) deep, where it provides an effective hiding place for wildfowl. (The non-variegated *Phragmites australis* is even more invasive and requires a lake.) The sturdy, upright, yellow-striped leaves grow 60cm (24in) long, and are topped by superb, 45cm (18in) long flowers held on even taller stems. The plumes are smaller than, but similar to, those of pampas grass (*Cortaderia selloana*), and make a magnificent sight when ruffled by the wind. An effective way of restricting the spread of 'Variegatus' is to grow it in a large underwater container.

PLANT PROFILE	
HEIGHT	2.5m (8ft)
SPREAD	Indefinite
SITE	Full sun
SOIL	Wet
HARDINESS	Fully hardy
FLOWERING	Late summer to mid-autumn

P *Phuopsis stylosa*

THIS SUMMER–LONG FLOWERING PERENNIAL needs to be grown at the foot of a wall or close to a path so that it can flop over and blur any straight edges with its straggling stems. It can even be used as ground cover on banks. Flowers are funnel-shaped and fragrant, and its leaves are narrow and grow in whorls. By cutting the plant back in the autumn, after flowering, it will become more compact and shapely. Grow this pale pink form with 'Purpurea' which has much richer pink flowers. Both retain their leaves through the autumn, and even into winter, until the temperatures start to dive. The soil needs to be free-draining.

PLANT PROFILE

HEIGHT 15cm (6in)

SPREAD 50cm (20in)

SITE Full sun or partial shade

SOIL Free-draining

HARDINESS Fully hardy

FLOWERING Summer

Physalis alkekengi var. *franchetii* Chinese lantern

P

THE BEST REASON for growing this plant is the amazing seedheads, not the creamy-white flowers that really don't amount to anything much. The seedheads look like small, red paper balls or lanterns (botanically known as calyces), with bright orange-scarlet berries within, and are used for cut-flower displays. The berries are edible, but eating any other part of the plant could give you an upset stomach. Extremely tolerant of a wide range of growing conditions, Chinese lanterns are happy in most gardens and require average soil that never becomes waterlogged or bakes dry. Wear gloves when handling the leaves because direct contact can irritate the skin.

OTHER VARIETY *P. alkekengi* (red lanterns).

PLANT PROFILE

HEIGHT 60–75cm (24–30in)

SPREAD 90cm (36in)

SITE Full sun or partial shade

SOIL Average, free-draining

HARDINESS Fully hardy

FLOWERING Midsummer

P

Physostegia virginiana var. *speciosa* 'Variegata' Obedient plant

A USEFUL COMPANION PLANT with a good show of flowers held on stiffly upright stems, this plant's common name comes from the fact that when the flowers are nudged to one side they do not bounce back. The plant makes a good-size clump of variegated foliage, and provides plenty of magenta-pink flowers for cutting from the middle of summer to early autumn. To do well it needs moist, rich soil and, in ideal conditions, will spread. 'Vivid' has stronger coloured, bright purple-pink flowers.

OTHER VARIETIES *P. virginiana* 'Bouquet Rose' (pale lilac-pink flowers); *P. virginiana* 'Summer Snow' (white and green flowers).

PLANT PROFILE
HEIGHT To 1.2m (4ft)
SPREAD 60cm (24in) or more
SITE Full sun or partial shade
SOIL Moist, fertile
HARDINESS Fully hardy
FLOWERING Midsummer to early autumn

Phytolacca americana Pokeweed

P

TALL, INVASIVE AND VERY POISONOUS, the pokeweed is a candidate for the wild garden, light woodland or even a streamside setting. The small white to pink flowers are followed by pokeweed's best feature – toxic, strikingly coloured, blackish-maroon berries. Despite the health warnings, it does make an impressive plant, large enough to become a summer hedge-like barrier; in the autumn, the foliage reddens up. All parts cause severe discomfort if eaten, and it should be kept out of gardens where children might be tempted by the berries, which can be lethal.

OTHER VARIETY *P. polyandra* (smaller-growing, purple-pink flowers, toxic black berries, leaves turn yellow in autumn).

PLANT PROFILE
HEIGHT To 4m (12ft)
SPREAD 1m (3ft)
SITE Full sun or partial shade
SOIL Moist, fertile
HARDINESS Fully hardy
FLOWERING Midsummer to early autumn

P | *Platycodon grandiflorus* Balloon flower

THE WAY THE FLOWER BUDS SWELL and swell, getting rounder and fatter until they open, gives this plant its common name of balloon flower. The flowers are 5cm (2in) wide, with dark blue veins and pointed tips, while the stems are not entirely sturdy, and do need staking to keep them upright. Provide rich, free-draining soil that does not dry out and bake in summer. *Platycodon* 'Mariesii' is a shorter, dark blue balloon flower that does not require staking.

OTHER VARIETIES *P. grandiflorus albus* (blue-veined white flowers); *P. grandiflorus* 'Apoyama' (deep violet flowers); *P. grandiflorus* 'Park's Double Blue' (double, violet-blue flowers); *P. grandiflorus* 'Perlmutterschale' (pale pink flowers).

PLANT PROFILE

HEIGHT	To 60cm (24in)
SPREAD	30cm (12in)
SITE Full sun or partial shade	
SOIL Fertile, free-draining	
HARDINESS Fully hardy	
FLOWERING Late summer	

Polemonium 'Lambrook Mauve' Jacob's ladder

P

THESE COTTAGE GARDEN FAVOURITES have a delicate quality, with flowers in lilac, blue, purple, pink, yellow, or white. The taller forms can be grown in borders; the shorter ones in rock or gravel gardens. Lilac-blue 'Lambrook Mauve' is an ideal choice for an informal bed, and needs average soil with well-rotted compost added to it to keep the ground moist. Deadhead promptly when the blooms have faded to eliminate seedlings and prolong the flowering season.

OTHER VARIETIES *P. caeruleum* (larger-growing, lavender-blue flowers); *P. caeruleum* subsp. *caeruleum* f. *album* (white flowers); *P. carneum* (smaller-growing, pale pink or yellow flowers); *P. pauciflorum* (red-tinted pale yellow flowers).

PLANT PROFILE
HEIGHT To 45cm (18in)
SPREAD To 45cm (18in)
SITE Full sun or partial shade
SOIL Average, moist
HARDINESS Fully hardy
FLOWERING Late spring and early summer

P | *Polygonatum* x *hybridum* 'Striatum' Solomon's seal

ONE OF THE BEST SPRING PLANTS, Solomon's seal hides itself away in shady corners or borders where each long, arching stem is adorned with a row of small, green-lipped, white, pendent flowers. These are followed by tiny, blue-black berries. The leaves feature thin, white stripes. Like other polygonatums, 'Striatum' spreads well to form attractive clumps where there is plenty of moist, rich soil. The flower stems can be cut for indoor displays.

OTHER VARIETIES *P. hookeri* (smaller-growing, pink flowers, black berries); *P. humile* (smaller-growing, white flowers, blue-black berries); *P. multiflorum* (smaller-growing, green-tipped white flowers, black berries); *P. odoratum* 'Flore Pleno' (double, green-tipped white flowers).

PLANT PROFILE
HEIGHT To 1.5m (5ft)
SPREAD 30cm (12in)
SITE Full or partial shade
SOIL Moist, fertile
HARDINESS Fully hardy
FLOWERING Late spring

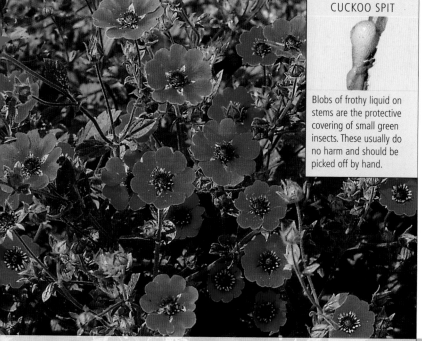

CUCKOO SPIT

Blobs of frothy liquid on stems are the protective covering of small green insects. These usually do no harm and should be picked off by hand.

Potentilla 'Gibson's Scarlet' Cinquefoil

P

BRIGHT TOMATO RED flowers add impact to any hot colour scheme. First come the rounded leaves, like those of a strawberry, then the flat circular blooms the size of small coins which keep appearing all summer on top of wiry, scrambling stems. It makes a vibrant show when planted next to a taller, wider, yellow-flowering potentilla, and also stands out next to a small, silver-beige grass. Average garden soil is fine; dig plenty of grit into heavy ground to improve drainage.

OTHER VARIETIES *P. aurea* (smaller-growing, golden-yellow flowers); *P. erecta* (smaller-growing, yellow flowers); *P.* 'Etna' (velvety red flowers); *P.* 'Gloire de Nancy' (double, reddish orange flowers); *P.* 'Monsieur Rouillard' (blood-red flowers with yellow marks).

PLANT PROFILE
HEIGHT To 45cm (18in)
SPREAD 60cm (24in)
SITE Full sun
SOIL Average, free-draining
HARDINESS Fully hardy
FLOWERING Early to late summer

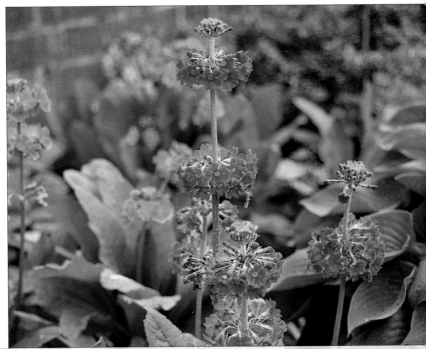

P

Primula beesiana Candelabra primula

ELEGANT AND EYE-CATCHING, this primula has a few long leaves at the base and a tall, thin, summer-flowering stem rising out of them. Dozens of tiny, bright reddish-purple flowers, each with a yellow eye, appear in clusters right up to the top. It needs moist, rich, neutral to acid soil (the type you would find in bog gardens), and will tolerate a sunny position provided the soil never dries out. The best time to divide established plants is in the spring.

OTHER VARIETIES *P. anisodora* (green-eyed brown-purple flowers); *P. aurantiaca* (smaller-growing, red-orange flowers); *P. bulleyana* (crimson flowers); *P. burmanica* (yellow-eyed red-purple flowers); *P.* 'Inverewe' (brilliant red flowers); *P. pulverulenta* (red-purple flowers).

PLANT PROFILE	
HEIGHT 60cm (24in)	
SPREAD 60cm (24in)	
SITE Partial shade	
SOIL Moist, fertile	
HARDINESS Fully hardy	
FLOWERING Summer	

Primula florindae Giant cowslip

THIS SUPERB PLANT is really worth growing, but you must provide it with wet ground right throughout the year, making it an obvious contender for a bog garden or the damp ground beside a stream. The flowering stems rise up out of the lush leaves and carry long-lasting clusters of about 40 pale yellow flowers. They are excellent for picking for an indoor display, where their gentle scent can be better appreciated. A sunny garden position is suitable only if the soil is moist throughout the year. Only a couple of plants are needed because they soon spread, forming magnificent clumps.

PLANT PROFILE	
HEIGHT	To 1.2m (4ft)
SPREAD	1m (3ft)
SITE	Partial shade
SOIL	Moist, fertile
HARDINESS	Fully hardy
FLOWERING	Summer

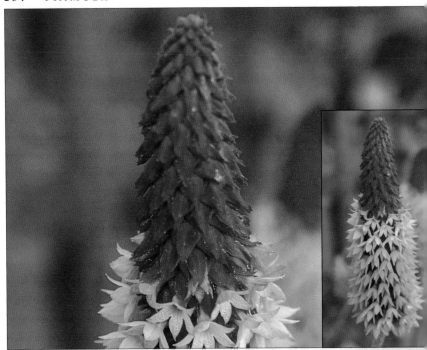

P

Primula vialii Primula

LOOKING LIKE A MINIATURE KNIPHOFIA (and often called the red hot poker primula), this is a highly attractive and distinctive plant. It initially has a two-tone cone on top of a short flower stem. From a distance, it looks as though the cone is bearing two different-coloured flowers – blue and red. In fact, it is the buds that are red and in early summer they open from the bottom of the cone to reveal tiny blue flowers. Since it has a reputation for being short-lived, it is best to collect seed after flowering, and then make sure the young seedlings are well watered. *Primula vialii* is suitable for bog gardens or the damp soil beside a stream.

PLANT PROFILE

HEIGHT 30–60cm (12–24in)

SPREAD 30cm (12in)

SITE Partial shade

SOIL Moist, fertile

HARDINESS Fully hardy

FLOWERING Summer

Prunella grandiflora 'Pink Loveliness' Self-heal

P

THE BEST POSSIBLE USE of 'Pink Loveliness' is as ground cover. It grows to form a thick covering of 10cm (4in) long leaves and, in summer, produces clear pink flowers on upright stems. The major advantage with this plant is that it will grow just about anywhere, from sunny to shady sites. It self-seeds unless sheared over as the flowers start to fade. Don't confuse it with the blue-purple *Prunella vulgaris*, which is grown in herb gardens and was traditionally used to heal external injuries and other ailments.

OTHER VARIETY *P. grandiflora* 'White Loveliness' (pure white flowers).

PLANT PROFILE
HEIGHT 15cm (6in)
SPREAD 1m (3ft)
SITE Full sun or partial shade
SOIL Average
HARDINESS Fully hardy
FLOWERING Summer

P

Pulmonaria 'Lewis Palmer' Lungwort

WITH ITS PINK FLOWERS in early spring that gradually turn bright blue, and long, white-spotted leaves, this plant has two main features. The leaves can grow up to 30cm (12in) long and fully develop after the plant has stopped flowering. It needs to be grown in light or deep shade in moist, rich soil, and makes good ground cover for a site close to deciduous trees. There is a wide choice of lungworts, some with white flowers (*Pulmonaria saccharata* 'Sissinghurst White'), others with red blooms (*P. rubra* 'Redstart').

OTHER VARIETIES *P. angustifolia* (rich blue flowers); *P.* 'Margery Fish' (smaller-growing, coral-pink flowers turning violet); *P. rubra* 'Bowles' Red' (coral-red flowers); *P. saccharata* 'Leopard' (red, pink-tinted flowers).

PLANT PROFILE

HEIGHT 35cm (14in)

SPREAD 45cm (18in)

SITE Light or deep shade

SOIL Moist, fertile

HARDINESS Fully hardy

FLOWERING Early spring

ROOT CUTTINGS

In winter, lift a vigorous plant. Cut a thick, healthy root close to the crown, and then into 5cm (2in) sections. Insert the roots vertically into pots of moist compost. The top ends of each cutting must be level with the surface.

Pulsatilla vulgaris Pasque flower

P

ATTRACTIVE PURPLE FLOWERS, some even white, held on short stems provide a fine spring show. The plant's requirement for excellent drainage and its diminutive size make it ideal for raised beds, a rock or gravel garden, the front of a border, or troughs. The silky flowers have an open bell shape with a yellow eye, and are followed in the summer by attractive seedheads. The white form is *Pulsatilla vulgaris alba*, 'Barton's Pink' is pink, and 'Röde Klokke' is deep red. Give each plant some space because it will grow to form a good-sized clump.

OTHER VARIETIES *P. halleri* (lavender-blue flowers); *P. vernalis* (smaller-growing, white flowers tinted bluish-violet).

PLANT PROFILE

HEIGHT	10–20cm (4–8in)
SPREAD	20cm (8in)
SITE	Full sun
SOIL	Free-draining
HARDINESS	Fully hardy
FLOWERING	Spring

R | *Ranunculus ficaria* 'Brazen Hussy' Lesser celandine

THIS TERRIFIC LITTLE BUTTERCUP has shiny brown leaves that offset the brash, bright yellow flowers. It grows naturally in woodland conditions where the soil is moist and rich, and the light varies from dappled sun to partial shade. 'Brazen Hussy' catches the eye when seen against gravel, where the full contrast between leaf and flower colour stands out, but it is also happy growing in wilder parts of the garden. Like most buttercups, it spreads well.

OTHER VARIETIES *R. acris* 'Flore Pleno' (larger-growing, double, yellow flowers); *R. bulbosus* 'F. M. Burton' (larger-growing, creamy-yellow flowers in autumn); *R. ficaria* 'Collarette' (double, yellow flowers, leaves with bronze bands); *R. gramineus* (larger-growing, lemon-yellow flowers).

PLANT PROFILE

HEIGHT 5cm (2in)

SPREAD 30cm (12in)

SITE Parial shade

SOIL Moist, fertile

HARDINESS Fully hardy

FLOWERING Early sprin.

Rehmannia elata Chinese foxglove

THE TUBULAR FLOWERS of this appropriately named plant look like those of a foxglove. This bushy perennial has dark green, 20cm (8in) long leaves, and in late spring and early summer vertical spires with flowers up to 10cm (4in) long. It is only just borderline hardy, and unless you can provide a sunny, frost-free site and free-draining soil it is best to lift the plant in autumn, cut it back and pot it up for overwintering in a cool greenhouse. Water the plant periodically to prevent the soil drying out completely, and put it outside again the following spring, after the frosts are over.

OTHER VARIETY *R. glutinosa* (smaller-growing, reddish-brown flowers with pale yellow-brown lips).

R

PLANT PROFILE
HEIGHT 1.5m (5ft)
SPREAD 50cm (20in)
SITE Full sun
SOIL Free-draining
HARDINESS Borderline hardy
FLOWERING Late spring to midsummer

R | *Rheum palmatum* 'Atrosanguineum' Chinese rhubarb

THIS IS A SPECIAL PLANT for a special place in the garden. In spring, the new, dramatic, rhubarb-like, jagged leaves are reddish-purple, and fade gradually to dark green. They're wonderfully large, reaching 90cm (36in) in length, and are accompanied by the vertical flower spikes, which are almost as impressive, with sprays of tiny crimson flowers. It makes a magnificent sight in moist soil by a pond but remember when placing this plant that it starts to die down in late summer and will need something close by to keep the show going.

OTHER VARIETIES   *R.* 'Ace of Hearts' (smaller-growing, pale pink to white flowers, red- and purple-veined leaves); *R. palmatum* (creamy-green to deep red flowers).

PLANT PROFILE
HEIGHT To 2.5m (8ft)
SPREAD To 2m (6ft)
SITE Full sun or partial shade
SOIL Moist, fertile
HARDINESS Fully hardy
FLOWERING Early summer

Rhodiola rosea Rosefoot

MAKING AN IMPRESSIVE FLOWERING CLUMP, which attracts bees and butterflies, rosefoot also has very attractive foliage. The leaves are almost oval and pointed, fleshy and bluish-grey, growing right the way up each strong stem, while the yellow flowers, with just a hint of green, are held at the very top. It is a good plant for a rock garden, or at the front of a raised bed or border, where it will be remarkably free-flowering. Avoid shade and heavy clay soil, and water it well in dry summer spells.

OTHER VARIETY *R. heterodonta* (larger-growing, star-shaped yellow flowers from red buds, male flowers with red or purple-red centres, greyish-green leaves).

PLANT PROFILE	
HEIGHT 5–30cm (2–12in)	
SPREAD 20cm (8in)	
SITE Full sun	
SOIL Fertile	
HARDINESS Fully hardy	
FLOWERING Summer	

R

Rodgersia pinnata 'Superba'

THIS PLANT HAS PLENTY OF IMPACT. It unfurls magnificent leaves, reaching up to 90cm (36in) long, that are bronze on opening in the spring, gradually turning dark green. In the summer they are topped by erect stems holding fluffy flowers that stay in good condition until mid-autumn. For the best display, plant it in moist, rich soil, out of the midsummer sun, and sheltered from winds. In a sunny site, use a thick mulch of compost to keep in the soil moisture. The new bronze foliage makes an effective contrast in a moist gravel bed.

OTHER VARIETIES *R. aesculifolia* (larger-growing, white or pink flowers); *R. podophylla* (larger-growing, creamy-green flowers, leaves bronze when young, bronze-red in autumn).

PLANT PROFILE

HEIGHT 1.2m (4ft)

SPREAD 75cm (30in)

SITE Sun or semi-shade

SOIL Moist, fertile

HARDINESS Fully hardy

FLOWERING Mid- and late summer

Rudbeckia 'Herbstonne' Coneflower

R

FOR HIGH-IMPACT SUMMER PLANTS for a border, coneflowers are ideal. 'Herbstonne' has large, bright yellow, daisy-like blooms with a brown cone in the middle. It makes a substantial clump and needs plenty of space. If it is too tall for your liking, you can pinch out the growing tips when the plant reaches about 75cm (30in) high. In windy gardens staking may be necessary. Add a thick spring mulch of compost, and water in dry weather to prevent plants becoming floppy. A shorter alternative is the similar *Rudbeckia fulgida* var. *sullivantii* 'Goldsturm' (black-eyed Susan).

OTHER VARIETIES *R. fulgida* var. *deamii* (shorter, orange-yellow flowers); *R. hirta* (shorter, golden-yellow flowers).

PLANT PROFILE	
HEIGHT 2m (6ft)	
SPREAD 90cm (36in)	
SITE Full sun or partial shade	
SOIL Fertile, free-draining	
HARDINESS Fully hardy	
FLOWERING Midsummer to early autumn	

S

Saccharum ravennae Ravenna grass

MAKING A SPECTACULAR SIGHT, this grass from the Mediterranean and North Africa has sword-like leaves that grow to about 90cm (36in) high, and have a tendency to arch over. Bursting out of the clumps of foliage are huge flower spikes topped by feathery plumes which initially have a pink tinge before turning silver. A good flower display does depend on a long, hot summer, however, and the soil should be average, rather than rich, and free-draining. It will grow just about anywhere in the garden – from borders to gravel gardens, or as a feature in its own special bed in a lawn – as long as it receives full sun. In cold-climate gardens, protect the crown of the plant in winter with horticultural fleece or a thick layer of bracken.

PLANT PROFILE

HEIGHT 2–3m (6–10ft)

SPREAD 1.2m (4ft)

SITE Full sun

SOIL Average, free-draining

HARDINESS Frost hardy

FLOWERING Late summer and autumn

Salvia patens Salvia

S

SUNNY BORDERS ARE ENHANCED by the rich, flamboyant colours and pale pastels of summer-flowering salvias. The deep blue *Salvia patens* is for the front of a border, while a taller, pale blue type is *S. uliginosa*, at 2m (6ft); the half-hardy *S. guaranitica* is nearly as tall with dark blue flowers, but it cannot be left in the open during winter. None of these salvias are totally hardy, and all need a sheltered site in full sun, good drainage, and a mulch of compost in frosty areas.

OTHER VARIETIES   *S. buchananii* (magenta-red flowers); *S. involucrata* (larger-growing, purplish-red flowers); *S. patens* 'Cambridge Blue' (pale blue flowers); *S. splendens* 'Red Riches' (smaller-growing, scarlet flowers); *S. x superba* (larger-growing, bright violet or purple flowers).

PLANT PROFILE
HEIGHT 45–60cm (18–24in)
SPREAD 45–60cm (18–24in)
SITE Full sun
SOIL Free-draining
HARDINESS Frost hardy
FLOWERING Midsummer to mid-autumn

S   *Salvia* x *sylvestris* 'Mainacht'

THIS HARDY SALVIA makes a colourful, bushy plant and is covered with indigo blue flowers throughout the summer, making it a good gap-filler for the front of a border, or a gravel garden. Alternatives include 'Rose Queen', which is rose-pink, while *Salvia* x *superba* is very similar to the different types of *S.* x *sylvestris* and equally hardy, with flowers in violet or purple. All need free-draining soil and full sun – avoid soil that's too rich as this encourages them to produce more leaves than flowers.

OTHER VARIETIES   *S. nemorosa* 'Ostfriesland' (smaller-growing, deep blue-violet flowers); *S.* x *sylvestris* 'Blauhügel' (smaller-growing, pure blue flowers); *S.* x *sylvestris* 'Rose Queen' (rose-pink flowers).

PLANT PROFILE
HEIGHT 70cm (28in)
SPREAD 45cm (18in)
SITE Full sun
SOIL Average, free-draining
HARDINESS Fully hardy
FLOWERING Early and midsummer

Sanguisorba obtusa Burnet

S

IF GARDEN SPACE IS TIGHT and you don't have room or the warm conditions for a large callistemon, then try this smaller perennial, which has beautiful, bottlebrush-like flowers. The flower spikes are 8cm (3in) long and held well clear of the bright, fresh green leaves. It is easy to grow provided the soil is fertile and free-draining but never dries out. It has a long flowering season and deserves a prominent position toward the front of a border or by a pond. Divide clumps in early spring to make more plants.

OTHER VARIETIES *S. canadensis* (larger-growing, spikes of fluffy white flowers); *S. officinalis* (larger-growing, dense spikes of small red-brown flowers).

PLANT PROFILE
HEIGHT To 60cm (24in)
SPREAD To 60cm (24in)
SITE Full sun or partial shade
SOIL Fertile, moist but free-draining
HARDINESS Fully hardy
FLOWERING Mid- or late summer to early autumn

S | *Saponaria ocymoides* Tumbling Ted

THE TOP OF A DRY-STONE WALL is perfect for this plant where the small pink summer flowers will tumble down the sides and show it off to the best effect. Its preference for free-draining conditions also makes it suitable for rock gardens, but beware of its quick-spreading habit. If it's too vigorous then try the red 'Rubra Compacta' which has a neater habit, or the white 'Alba'. They can all be cut back after flowering to restrict their spread, and to keep the plants neat.

OTHER VARIETIES *S.* 'Bressingham' (deep pink flowers); *S. officinalis* (larger-growing, pink, red, or white flowers); *S. officinalis* 'Alba Plena' (double, white flowers); *S. x olivana* (smaller-growing, pale pink flowers).

PLANT PROFILE

HEIGHT 8cm (3in)

SPREAD 45cm (18in)

SITE Full sun

SOIL Free-draining

HARDINESS Fully hardy

FLOWERING Summer

Scabiosa atropurpurea 'Chile Black' Pincushion flower

S

COMBINING WELL WITH silver-leaved plants, bright green leaves and flashy red dahlias, 'Chile Black' has small, dark red flowers (looking almost black from a distance) with white flecks. Grow it in an average soil with excellent drainage in a border or a gravel garden where the stones provide a foil for its dark flowers. Although short-lived, *Scabiosa atropurpurea* 'Ace of Spades' is a fine alternative with equally deep crimson flowers, blooming well into winter in sheltered gardens.

OTHER VARIETIES *S.* 'Butterfly Blue' (smaller-growing, lavender-blue flowers); *S. caucasica* 'Miss Wilmott' (larger-growing, white flowers); *S. graminifolia* 'Pinkushion' (smaller-growing, rose-pink flowers).

PLANT PROFILE
HEIGHT 60cm (24in)
SPREAD 60cm (24in)
SITE Full sun
SOIL Average, free-draining
HARDINESS Fully hardy
FLOWERING Mid- and late summer

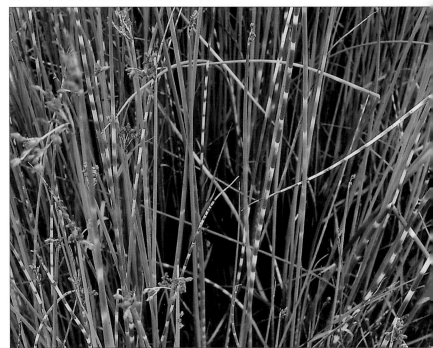

S | *Schoenoplectus lacustris* subsp. *tabernaemontani* 'Zebrinus' Club-rush

THIS TYPE OF BULRUSH is for boggy, moist, neutral to acid soil found at the edge of a large pond, lake or stream. 'Zebrinus' has upright, graceful, thin, grey-green stems, with highly distinctive horizontal creamy-white bands which make it among the most spectacular of the rushes. The brown flowers are insignificant. Note that this rush is sometimes listed as *Scirpus* instead of *Schoenoplectus*. Other excellent varieties include the virtually white-stemmed 'Albescens' and the yellow-stemmed 'Golden Spears'.

PLANT PROFILE	
HEIGHT 1m (3ft)	
SPREAD 60cm (24in)	
SITE Full sun	
SOIL Wet	
HARDINESS Fully hardy	
FLOWERING Early to late summer	

Scrophularia auriculata 'Variegata' Water figwort

S

A PRIME CONTENDER FOR BOG GARDENS, the shallows in a pond or very moist borders, 'Variegata' has attractive leaves with broad, creamy-white margins. Since the flowers are not particularly exciting, you can remove the flower stems and allow the plant to put all its energy into more leaf production, or cut them off the moment they start to fade. 'Variegata' can be grown among the likes of *Myosotis* (water forget-me-nots) and *Lysichiton americanus* (skunk cabbage). If you are growing it in the shallows of a pond, it likes to be planted at a depth of about 15cm (6in).

OTHER VARIETY *S. auriculata* (yellowish-green flowers, wrinkled, toothed, dark green leaves).

PLANT PROFILE
HEIGHT 90cm (36in)
SPREAD 90cm (36in)
SITE Dappled to partial shade
SOIL Wet
HARDINESS Fully hardy
FLOWERING Early summer to early autumn

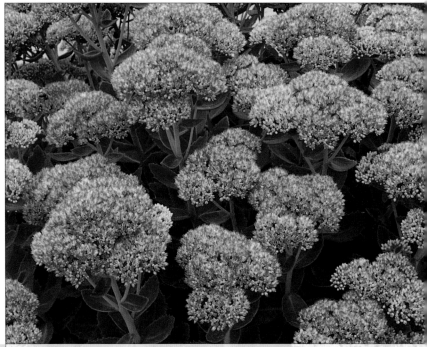

S | *Sedum 'Herbstfreude'* Stonecrop

IMPARTING A VALUABLE DASH of pink, white or purple flowers to the autumn garden, the taller sedums have the added bonus of attracting peacock butterflies and bees. 'Herbstfreude' has deep pink flowers that gradually acquire a bronze tint, and end up dark copper-red. Sedums are succulents with attractive fleshy leaves, and can be grown in borders and around ponds, away from the moist edges, in average soil with good drainage. Divide them in the autumn, after flowering, by slicing off a section with some roots attached.

OTHER VARIETIES *S. spectabile* 'Brilliant' (smaller-growing, pink flowers); *S. telephium* subsp. *maximum* 'Atropurpureum' (pink flowers with orange centres); *S. telephium* 'Munstead Red' (red flowers).

PLANT PROFILE
HEIGHT 60cm (24in)
SPREAD 60cm (24in)
SITE Full sun
SOIL Average, free-draining
HARDINESS Fully hardy
FLOWERING Early autumn

Selinum wallichianum

S

COTTAGE GARDENS, INFORMAL BORDERS and wild gardens are all excellent sites for this plant (which looks a little like cow parsley), although an immaculate formal border may not be the best position. The multi-branched stems have fern-like leaves and are topped by tiny, star-shaped, white flowers. Both the flowers and the foliage enliven cut-flower displays. In the wild, it is often found growing on rocky slopes and mountain meadows in Europe and the Himalayas, and needs similar good drainage and average soil in the garden. Take care to find the perfect position when planting because it resents being moved once it is in the ground and established.

PLANT PROFILE	
HEIGHT To 2m (6ft)	
SPREAD 60cm (24in)	
SITE Full sun or partial shade	
SOIL Average, free-draining	
HARDINESS Fully hardy	
FLOWERING Midsummer to early autumn	

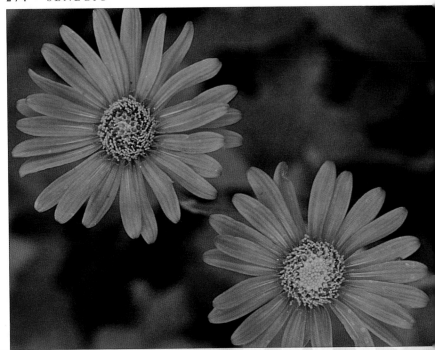

S

Senecio pulcher

THIS IS A PLANT WITH A DIFFERENCE. Most senecios have yellow, daisy-like flowers but this South American species has sprays of almost magenta-mauve blooms with prominent yellow eyes, and is good enough to be the star plant in any group. It requires soil with good drainage, and because it is not totally hardy it needs a sunny, sheltered position in the garden. In cold-climate gardens you can dig up *Senecio pulcher*, cut it back, and pot it up for overwintering in a cool greenhouse.

OTHER VARIETIES *S. smithii* (larger-growing, white flowers with yellow centres, moisture-loving); *S. tanguticus* (larger-growing, bright yellow flowers, invasive).

PLANT PROFILE
HEIGHT 45–60cm (18–24in)
SPREAD 50cm (20in)
SITE Full sun
SOIL Free-draining
HARDINESS Frost hardy
FLOWERING Mid- and late autumn

Sidalcea 'Elsie Heugh'

S

LIKE A SHORTER VERSION of a hollyhock, 'Elsie Heugh' has open flowers ranged towards the top of vertical spires that tower above the foliage. The rich pink 'Elsie Heugh' is a gem for cottage gardens or formal borders where it adds a gentle, summery note. Other colours are in the reddish-pink to soft pink range. Sidalceas grow in most sunny gardens with fertile soil. Cut back the stems once the flowers have finished and you should be rewarded with a second flush of flowers toward autumn.

OTHER VARIETIES *S. candida* (smaller-growing, white or cream flowers); *S.* 'Croftway Red' (reddish-pink flowers); *S.* 'William Smith' (deep rose-pink flowers with salmon-pink tints).

PLANT PROFILE	
HEIGHT 90cm (36in)	
SPREAD 45cm (18in)	
SITE Full sun	
SOIL Fertile, moist but free-draining	
HARDINESS Fully hardy	
FLOWERING Early and midsummer	

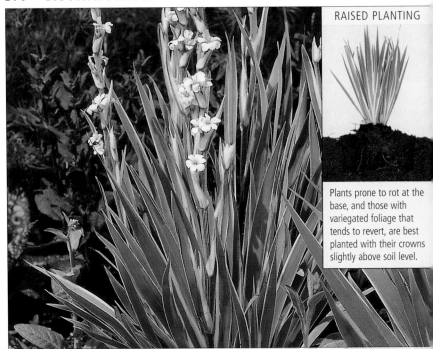

RAISED PLANTING

Plants prone to rot at the base, and those with variegated foliage that tends to revert, are best planted with their crowns slightly above soil level.

S

Sisyrinchium striatum 'Aunt May'

WITH VERTICAL, SWORD-SHAPED, variegated leaves about 40cm (16in) long, and stiff flower spikes with pale yellow flowers, 'Aunt May' is a very striking plant. The fan of evergreen leaves has an architectural symmetry and needs to be planted where it can be seen clearly in free-draining soil with average fertility. Its parent, *Sisyrinchium striatum*, has plain green leaves. The semi-evergreen, 50cm (20in) high *S. graminoides* has blue flowers and all varieties look good in gravel gardens.

OTHER VARIETIES *S.* 'Biscutella' (smaller-growing, heavily veined, dull yellow flowers); *S. californicum* (dark-veined, bright yellow flowers, grey-green leaves); *S. idahoense* 'Album' (smaller-growing, white flowers).

PLANT PROFILE

HEIGHT To 50cm (20in)

SPREAD 25cm (10in)

SITE Full sun

SOIL Average, free-draining

HARDINESS Fully hardy

FLOWERING Early and midsummer

Smilacina racemosa False spikenard

S

THE FLUFFY WHITE FLOWERS of false spikenard appear in clusters at the ends of arching stems – not dangling right the way along them as with Solomon's seal, to which this plant is sometimes likened. Being a woodland plant with spring flowers, it is perfect for shady, damp, rich soil, where it will form large clumps. The blooms can be used for cut-flower displays in the spring, or in autumn, when tiny green berries that ripen to red appear. Established clumps can be divided in the spring to create extra plants but make sure each division has its own set of roots.

OTHER VARIETY *S. stellata* (tiny white, star-like flowers on arching stems, similar to *S. racemosa*).

PLANT PROFILE
HEIGHT 90cm (36in)
SPREAD 60cm (24in)
SITE Dappled or deep shade
SOIL Moist, fertile
HARDINESS Fully hardy
FLOWERING Mid- and late spring

S

Soldanella minima Least snowbell

THE LEAVES OF THIS PLANT are attractively rounded or heart-shaped, and the flower stems that rise through the foliage have downward-pointing, bell-shaped, pale blue (sometimes white) flowers. Possible problems arise because the plant dislikes excessive winter wet (it can be potted up and kept in a cool greenhouse from the end of autumn to the following spring), and slugs and snails attack the new growth. To help alleviate both problems, apply a layer of grit over the soil surface. This facilitates drainage and deters slugs, which dislike the sharp surface.

OTHER VARIETIES *S. alpina* (bluish-violet flowers); *S. carpatica* (violet-blue flowers); *S. villosa* (larger-growing, violet flowers).

PLANT PROFILE	
HEIGHT 10cm (4in)	
SPREAD 20cm (8in)	
SITE Full sun	
SOIL Free-draining	
HARDINESS Fully hardy	
FLOWERING Early spring	

Soleirolia soleirolii Baby's tears

MAKING INCREDIBLY EFFECTIVE ground cover, this plant quickly sends out a thin, fast-spreading mat of small, fresh green leaves and will colonize any spare piece of ground, whether it is a bank or an area beneath trees. Baby's tears is tolerant of a wide range of soil conditions and will grow in either sun or shade. It is cut back by the frost, but quickly recovers the following spring. Make sure you really do want baby's tears in your garden before planting it – once it takes hold, eradication is virtually impossible. Other varieties may be difficult to find.

OTHER VARIETIES   *S. soleirolii* 'Aurea' (golden-green leaves); *S. soleirolii* 'Variegata' (leaves with silver markings).

PLANT PROFILE	
HEIGHT 5cm (2in)	
SPREAD Indefinite	
SITE Sun or shade	
SOIL Average	
HARDINESS Fully hardy	
FLOWERING Summer	

S Solidago 'Goldenmosa' Golden rod

THIS IS A VIGOROUS, LATE-SUMMER PLANT, and a good choice for lovers of bright yellow. It makes a bushy clump in borders or wild gardens, and you can use its multiplying tendency to create gradually spreading drifts. 'Golden Wings' is a tall alternative, at nearly 2m (6ft) high, while *Solidago virgaurea* subsp. *alpestris* var. *minutissima* is one of the shortest, growing from 5–20cm (2–8in) high. All varieties prefer free-draining, sandy soil and full sun. One possible problem with this plant is powdery mildew, which can be reduced by watering the plant during the growing period.

OTHER VARIETY *S.* 'Crown of Rays' (shorter, golden-yellow flowers in flattened heads).

PLANT PROFILE

HEIGHT To 75cm (30in)

SPREAD 45cm (18in)

SITE Full sun

SOIL Average, free-draining

HARDINESS Fully hardy

FLOWERING Late summer and early autumn

x *Solidaster luteus* 'Lemore'

S

WITH ITS BRIGHT MASS of lemon-yellow, daisy-like flowers, this perennial looks good when planted toward the front of a border where it adds pastel shades through the second half of summer and into the autumn. Darker, more intense adjacent colours provide an effective contrast, bringing out its gentle hue. The flowers' also add an attractive note to a cut-flower arrangement. Soil with average fertility is perfectly acceptable but good drainage is important, as is plenty of bright sun. 'Lemore' is sometimes prone to powdery mildew, but this can be prevented by watering during the growing season or treating it with an appropriate fungicide spray.

PLANT PROFILE

HEIGHT 80cm (32in)

SPREAD 80cm (32in)

SITE Full sun

SOIL Average, free-draining

HARDINESS Fully hardy

FLOWERING Midsummer to early autumn

Spartina pectinata 'Aureomarginata'

IF YOU HAVE A PIECE OF SPARE GROUND near a pond then this spreading, but easily controllable, grass may be for you. It thrives in moist soil, where it makes mounds of glossy, thin, olive-green leaves with yellow stripes. It can also be grown on other sites provided the soil does not dry out; away from wet ground its spread is reduced. The straw-coloured flowers appear on tall spires and gradually turn brown, but the best reason for including this plant in a scheme is its autumn foliage, which flares up yellow before fading to beige for the winter. If space permits, grow it in drifts – for example, by the edge of a stream – or in a coastal location, as it is tolerant of salt.

OTHER VARIETY *S. pectinata* (green leaves).

PLANT PROFILE

HEIGHT 1.2m (4ft)

SPREAD Indefinite

SITE Full sun

SOIL Wet

HARDINESS Fully hardy

FLOWERING Autumn

Stachys byzantina Lamb's ears

S

SOFT, SILKY AND SILVERY-GREY, the leaves of this plant look and feel just like lambs' ears. Although the description of pink-purple flowers sounds attractive, in reality the blooms are not spectacular and many gardeners remove the flower stems to prevent them detracting from the foliage. Provide free-draining, average garden soil and full sun. *Stachys byzantina* 'Silver Carpet' is a good alternative because it very rarely flowers and the leaves have a strong silvery tinge.

OTHER VARIETIES *S. byzantina* 'Big Ears' (large, greyish-white felted mid-green leaves); *S. byzantina* 'Cotton Boll' (clusters of modified flowers looking like balls of cotton wool); *S. byzantina* 'Primrose Heron' (yellowish-grey leaves).

PLANT PROFILE
HEIGHT 45cm (18in)
SPREAD 60cm (24in)
SITE Full sun
SOIL Average, free-draining
HARDINESS Fully hardy
FLOWERING Early summer to early autumn

S

Stipa calamagrostis Feather grass

THIS IS ONE OF THE BEST GRASSES for any medium-size garden. In summer, feather grass is beautifully graceful with silvery flowers light enough to catch a passing breeze. By the end of the summer, the flowers have changed to fawn, and a few weeks later, in autumn, the foliage turns yellow and stays evergreen until the really cold nights set in. It is also a wonderfully tactile plant and is best grown where you can flick it with your fingers as you pass, and use the flowers for cut-flower displays. Light, free-draining soil gives the best results.

OTHER VARIETIES *S. arundinacea* (feathery dark green leaves, streaked orange-brown); *S. gigantea* (larger-growing, silvery purplish-green flower spikes turning gold).

PLANT PROFILE	
HEIGHT 1m (3ft)	
SPREAD 1.2m (4ft)	
SITE Full sun	
SOIL Fertile, free-draining	
HARDINESS Fully hardy	
FLOWERING Summer	

Strobilanthes attenuata

S

GROWN FOR ITS QUIRKILY ATTRACTIVE, tubular-shaped flowers, about 4cm (1½in) long, this Indian perennial can be made even bushier by pinching out the growing tips in the spring. The indigo or purple flower colour looks slightly richer and darker when seen in light shade. The soil needs to be light and free-draining for the plant to thrive and, although hardy, in cold-climate gardens it needs the protection of a thick cover of bracken around the plant in the winter. Most other *Strobilanthes* are tender and need to be grown in a cool greenhouse over winter – they can then be placed outside in the summer when the last frosts have finished.

PLANT PROFILE
HEIGHT 1.2m (4ft)
SPREAD 1m (3ft)
SITE Full sun or partial shade
SOIL Free-draining
HARDINESS Fully hardy
FLOWERING Summer

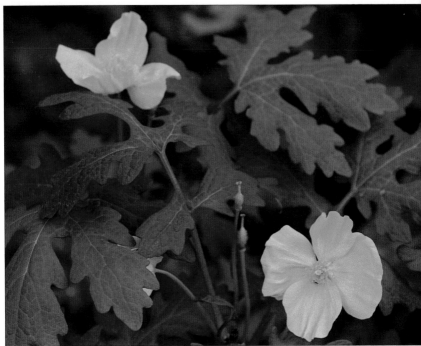

S

Stylophorum diphyllum Celandine poppy

THIS IS A BEAUTIFUL POPPY with distinctive and attractive, five- to seven-fingered leaves, which can grow to 30cm (12in) in length, and small yellow or orange flowers. While most poppies are sun-lovers, this type prefers moist but free-draining, leafy soil at the edge of a group of trees, or in a shrub border where it will benefit from some light shade. You can propagate it by collecting seed or by dividing large clumps in the autumn. Sometimes the pale yellow *Stylophorum lasiocarpum* is also sold in nurseries, but it is quite short-lived.

PLANT PROFILE

HEIGHT 30cm (12in)

SPREAD 30cm (12in)

SITE Partial shade

SOIL Moist but free-draining

HARDINESS Fully hardy

FLOWERING Late spring and summer

Symphyandra wanneri

S

WITH FLOWERS A LITTLE LIKE those of a campanula (bellflower) to which it is related, this high-value plant produces a good show of dark violet-blue blooms in summer. Sometimes taking a few years to flower, it often then dies but scatters so much seed that there will be plenty of replacements for the following spring. Move young plants to any gaps in the border where, being just knee high or less, they need to be placed toward the front. Light, free-draining soil is best, but note that new growth acts as a magnet to slugs and snails.

OTHER VARIETIES *S. armena* (larger-growing, white or pale blue flowers); *S. hofmannii* (larger-growing, white to cream flowers); *S. pendula* (larger-growing, creamy-white flowers).

PLANT PROFILE	
HEIGHT 30cm (12in)	
SPREAD 30cm (12in)	
SITE Full sun or light shade	
SOIL Free-draining	
HARDINESS Fully hardy	
FLOWERING Summer	

S

Symphytum 'Goldsmith' Comfrey

IN THE WILDER PARTS of the garden, where the soil is moist and heavy, comfrey produces flowering, quick-spreading ground cover. Keep it out of formal borders, however, or it will overwhelm its neighbours. 'Goldsmith' has rich green leaves with cream and yellow or gold markings. Its foliage is so good, in fact, that this feature is more valued than the flowers. Once the flowers have faded, shear over the plant to promote a second flush of leaves.

OTHER VARIETIES *S. caucasicum* (larger-growing, bright blue flowers, lance-shaped mid-green leaves); *S.* 'Hidcote Blue' (larger-growing, pale blue flowers from red buds, mid-green leaves); *S.* 'Hidcote Pink' (pale pink and white flowers, mid-green leaves).

PLANT PROFILE
HEIGHT 30cm (12in)
SPREAD 30cm (12in)
SITE Full sun or partial shade
SOIL Moist
HARDINESS Fully hardy
FLOWERING Mid- and l spring

Tanacetum coccineum 'James Kelway'

T

HELD HIGH ABOVE this plant's finely divided foliage are superb, rich crimson, daisy-like flowers, each with a yellow eye. It offers a first-rate display in early-summer borders, needing only bright sun and average soil to succeed, although the ground should be more on the light and free-draining side. Promptly deadhead fading flowers to encourage a second flush later in the summer. Excellent alternatives include the cerise-pink 'Brenda', pink 'Eileen May Robinson' and white 'Snow Cloud'.

OTHER VARIETIES *T. balsamita* (larger-growing, white flowers with yellow eyes); *T. parthenium* (smaller-growing, yellow and white flowers); *T. vulgare* (smaller-growing, clusters of bright yellow flowers).

PLANT PROFILE
HEIGHT 60cm (24in)
SPREAD 45cm (18in)
SITE Full sun
SOIL Average, free-draining
HARDINESS Fully hardy
FLOWERING Early summer

T | *Telekia speciosa*

THIS IS A GOOD FUN, spreading perennial with rather limp leaves 30cm (12in) long, and tall stems bearing shaggy, daisy-like flowers. *Telekia speciosa* is generally considered much too ungainly for the more manicured border, but it is extremely useful in cottage-style and wild gardens, as well as on the banks of streams, because it self-seeds so freely. It forms clumps, and can be positioned as a surprise feature in unlikely places – as a backdrop to the cardoon (*Cynara cardunculus*), for example – or in shady corners of the garden. Provide moist soil and some shelter in exposed, windy gardens, and take precautions against slugs.

PLANT PROFILE

HEIGHT To 2m (6ft)

SPREAD 1m (3ft)

SITE Partial shade

SOIL Moist

HARDINESS Fully hardy

FLOWERING Late summe
and early autumn

Tellima grandiflora Fringe cups

T

HAPPY IN WOODLAND CONDITIONS, where self-seeding produces good ground cover, as well as in the drier parts of a shrub border, this is a dual-purpose plant. It has oval leaves, up to 10cm (4in) wide, with tall stems of tiny greenish-white flowers growing toward the top. These open from small, tight buds to give an open, airy display. Carefully dig up the seedlings in the spring and plant them close together to create a clump of five or six plants in moist but free-draining soil.

OTHER VARIETY *T. grandiflora* 'Purpurteppich' (smaller-growing, pink-fringed green flowers, green leaves flushed purple-red).

PLANT PROFILE
HEIGHT To 80cm (32in)
SPREAD 30cm (12in)
SITE Partial shade
SOIL Moist, free-draining
HARDINESS Fully hardy
FLOWERING Late spring to midsummer

T

Thalictrum aquilegiifolium Meadow rue

A SHOW OF DAINTY LEAVES and tiny, fluffy flowers (without petals) on angular stems give meadow rue an airy appearance. Rather than making a visual barrier, you can see through the plant's open tracery, so try placing it more toward the front of a border with contrasting coloured plants behind. If a similar effect is required for the second-half of summer, try *Thalictrum delavayi* 'Hewitt's Double' which has long-lasting mauve flowers. Moist soil is best for all meadow rues.

OTHER VARIETIES *T. aquilegiifolium* var. *album* (white flowers); *T. aquilegiifolium* 'Thundercloud' (dark-purple flowers); *T. flavum* subsp. *glaucum* (sulphur-yellow flowers, blue-grey leaves); *T. rochebruneanum* (white or lavender-pink flowers).

PLANT PROFILE	
HEIGHT To 1m (3ft)	
SPREAD 45cm (18in)	
SITE Partial shade	
SOIL Moist	
HARDINESS Fully hardy	
FLOWERING Early summer	

Thalictrum flavum subsp. *glaucum* Yellow meadow rue

T

WITH ITS OPEN, AIRY STEMS and aerial show of tiny flowers, this meadow rue very is similar to *Thalictrum aquilegiifolium*. It is a good plant for the middle of a border in a cottage-style garden, or for a wild area or the dappled shade beneath deciduous trees. A dark background helps to show off the clouds of yellow flowers, but if there is anything behind it that has a similar colour, then the hazy effect will be immediately lost. Plant it in moist soil that doesn't dry out, and divide clumps in the spring.

OTHER VARIETIES *T. delavayi* 'Album' (larger-growing, white flowers); *T. flavum* (fragrant, yellow and white flowers).

PLANT PROFILE

HEIGHT To 1m (3ft)	
SPREAD 60cm (24in)	
SITE Partial shade	
SOIL Moist	
HARDINESS Fully hardy	
FLOWERING Summer	

T

Thermopsis rhombifolia var. *montana* False lupin

THE EARLY SUMMER BUZZ OF BEES accompanies the flowering of this plant, which has yellow, lupin-like blooms and three-fingered leaves. It is a bright, invasive plant and needs to be restricted to wild gardens – in a border, it will attempt to take over all available space. For a taller version, try the yellow-flowering *Thermopsis villosa*. Its blooms open slightly earlier, from the end of spring. Both are tough and sturdy survivors, tolerating a range of different garden sites and soils, although free-draining ground is best. Take care when planning its position because it does not like being moved once established.

OTHER VARIETY   *L. villosa* (taller-growing, downy-yellow flowers, blue-grey leaves).

PLANT PROFILE

HEIGHT 90cm (36in)

SPREAD 60cm (24in)

SITE Full sun or partial shade

SOIL Free-draining

HARDINESS Fully hardy

FLOWERING Early summer

Tiarella cordifolia Foam flower

T

PRODUCING A BOLD SHOW of 10cm (4in) long leaves, through which tall, thin stems appear holding creamy-white flowers, this perennial is at its best in moist, fertile ground. In the wild, it is found in large colonies in woodlands where it spreads by underground stems, and it suits a similar site in the garden, wild areas or a position close to natural ponds. *Tiarella wherryi* is more compact and a better choice for a smaller garden, while *T. wherryi* 'Bronze Beauty' offers an exciting contrast between its white flowers and dark reddish-bronze leaves.

OTHER VARIETY *T.* 'Martha Oliver' (white flowers, leaves with maroon markings).

PLANT PROFILE
HEIGHT 10–30cm (4–12in)
SPREAD To 30cm (12in)
SITE Deep or light shade
SOIL Moist, fertile
HARDINESS Fully hardy
FLOWERING Late spring to midsummer

T

Tradescantia Andersoniana Group 'Osprey'

EASILY GROWN AND CREATING COLOURFUL DRIFTS, this is a clump-forming, hardy perennial (sometimes called spiderwort). Although sharing the same name, it is nothing like the trailing tradescantias popularly grown as houseplants. Grow it either in a single-colour group or combine it with the dark blue 'Isis', whitish, pale blue 'Iris Pritchard', red 'Karminglut' or 'Purple Dome'. All are easily grown in moist but free-draining soil. If the soil is too rich there will be an abundance of lax, soft growth and fewer flowers.

OTHER VARIETIES   (all Andersoniana Group) 'J.C. Weguelin' (large pale blue flowers); 'Purewell Giant' (smaller-growing, large purple to rose-red flowers); 'Zwanenburg Blue' (large dark blue flowers).

PLANT PROFILE

HEIGHT 60cm (24in)

SPREAD 45cm (18in)

SITE Sun or light shade

SOIL Moist, free-draining

HARDINESS Fully hardy

FLOWERING Early summer to early autumn

Tricyrtis formosana Toad lily

T

THIS PLANT IS EXQUISITE and needs a position at the front of the border. The six small, open petals have beautiful markings, with tiny purple spots on a white background, and an erect, fleshy middle. Despite their exotic look, toad lilies are easy to grow and given moist, rich soil they will spread to form decent groups. There are a few different types to choose from, all with different coloured markings. Toad lilies dislike being moved once they are in the ground, and you will need to keep a close watch for slugs and snails.

OTHER VARIETIES *S. hirta* 'Alba' (green-flushed white flowers with pink-tinged centres); *S. hirta* 'Miyazaki' (white flowers with lilac-purple spots); *T. macrantha* (deep yellow flowers with red-brown spots).

PLANT PROFILE	
HEIGHT To 80cm (32in)	
SPREAD 45cm (18in)	
SITE Deep or partial shade	
SOIL Moist, fertile	
HARDINESS Fully hardy	
FLOWERING Early autumn	

T | *Trifolium repens* 'Purpurascens Quadrifolium' Clover

WITH ITS SEMI-EVERGREEN, BI-COLOURED leaves, purple-maroon in the middle and green right around the margins, this is a very special form of clover. It has an incredibly invasive nature, however, which means that the wildfower garden is the only place it can be safely grown. Don't be tempted to put it in your ornamental lawn – if you do, the smooth green grass will be quickly colonized by scores of maroon blobs. In summer it produces small, rounded white flowers.

OTHER VARIETIES *T. pratense* 'Susan Smith' (larger-growing, leaves with gold, vein-like markings); *T. repens* 'Green Ice' (grey-green leaves with a darker centre); *T. repens* 'Purpurascens' (chocolate-brown foliage, white flowers); *T. repens* 'Wheatfen'(maroon flowers and leaves).

PLANT PROFILE

HEIGHT To 10cm (4in)

SPREAD Indefinite

SITE Full sun

SOIL Moist but free-draining

HARDINESS Fully hardy

FLOWERING Summer

Trillium grandiflorum Wake robin

T

A GARDEN AREA WITH MOIST SOIL and dappled shade offers the perfect conditions for this ground cover plant. The leaves grow to 30cm (12in) long, and the yellow-eyed flowers, which gradually turn pink, sit flush with the top of the foliage. Enrich the ground with annual additions of leaf mould for the best results. *Trillium erectum* grows slightly taller and has deep reddish-purple spring flowers (sometimes white or yellow). *T. sessile* is 30cm (12in) high with red-maroon flowers and 12cm (5in) long leaves.

OTHER VARIETIES *T. erectum* f. *albiflorum* (white or pale pink flowers); *T. grandiflorum* 'Flore Pleno' (double, white flowers); *T. luteum* (gold- or bronze-green flowers).

PLANT PROFILE

HEIGHT To 40cm (16in)

SPREAD 30cm (12in)

SITE Deep or partial shade

SOIL Moist, fertile

HARDINESS Fully hardy

FLOWERING Spring and summer

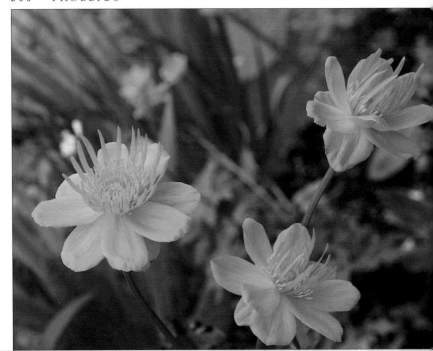

T

Trollius chinensis 'Golden Queen' Globeflower

SOME OF THE BEST FLOWERS for the spring and early summer are provided by globeflowers with their buttercup-like yellow or orange blooms, held on long thin stems. 'Golden Queen' flowers slightly later than most, and has rich orange flowers, 5cm (2in) wide, with long petals. Other types also have excellent colours, such as the early spring-flowering *Trollius* x *cultorum* 'Earliest of All' (yellow), and the late-spring 'Feuertroll' (rich orange-yellow). All like boggy, wet soil near a pond, or damp ground in a border.

OTHER VARIETIES *T.* x *cultorum* 'Alabaster' (primrose-yellow flowers); *T.* x *cultorum* 'Lemon Queen' (pale yellow flowers); *T. europaeus* (lemon-yellow flowers); *T. pumilus* (smaller-growing, gold-yellow flowers).

PLANT PROFILE

HEIGHT To 90cm (36in)

SPREAD 45cm (18in)

SITE Full sun or partial shade

SOIL Wet

HARDINESS Fully hardy

FLOWERING Midsummer

Tulbaghia violacea Wild garlic

T

THIS GORGEOUS PLANT, with narrow, strap-shaped leaves, and slim stems bearing up to 20 star-like flowers, requires quite specific conditions. Originating from South Africa, it needs a sunny, sheltered position and moderately rich soil with very good drainage. In cold-climate gardens you should dig it up in autumn and keep it potted in a cool greenhouse until the following spring. Although not a member of the garlic family, its characteristic smell gives rise to its common name of wild garlic. An alternative is *Tulbaghia violacea* 'Silver Lace' which has cream-coloured striped leaves and larger flowers. Both types grow into attractive clumps.

OTHER VARIETY *T. simmleri* (fragrant, deep purple flowers).

PLANT PROFILE
HEIGHT 45–60cm (18–24in)
SPREAD 25cm (10in)
SITE Full sun
SOIL Free-draining
HARDINESS Frost hardy
FLOWERING Midsummer to early autumn

U | *Uncinia rubra* Hook sedge

NATIVE TO THE MOUNTAINS of New Zealand, this evergreen sedge has narrow, slow-growing, reddish-brown leaves that are at their most attractive in the spring and early summer. It develops into a decent clump, but the flowers are totally insignificant, not least because they are the same colour as the foliage. The seed of the hook sedge is interesting, though, as each one has a tiny hook that latches onto any passing animal, thereby aiding dispersion. You can grow hook sedge in a sunny position and moist but well-drained soil, perhaps close to a natural pond.

OTHER VARIETY *U. uncinata* (pale brown to red-brown, flat, leaves with rough margins, spikes of dark brown flowers).

PLANT PROFILE

HEIGHT 30cm (12in)

SPREAD 35cm (14in)

SITE Full sun or light shade

SOIL Moist but free-draining

HARDINESS Frost hardy

FLOWERING Mid- and late summer

Uvularia grandiflora Merrybells

U

A NORTH AMERICAN WOODLAND PLANT, merrybells happily makes the transition to garden conditions and thrives if provided with rich, moist but well-drained soil. It is ideal for an area close to a natural pond, where it will form open clumps and provide a good place for toads and frogs to hide. It can also be grown in borders, but the soil must be moist with plenty of leafmould added to it. In mid-spring, merrybells is topped by downward-pointing, 5cm (2in) long, yellow flowers. Beware of attacks from slugs and snails when the new, fresh green growth emerges in the early spring.

PLANT PROFILE
HEIGHT 75cm (30in)
SPREAD 30cm (12in)
SITE Deep or partial shade
SOIL Fertile, moist but free-draining
HARDINESS Fully hardy
FLOWERING Mid- and late spring

V

Valeriana phu 'Aurea' **Valerian**

IN SPRING THIS PLANT DELIVERS A LOVELY SURPRISE, when its young foliage emerges a buttery yellow. After this eye-catching show, the leaves mature to lime green then mid-green by summer. To achieve the brightest possible spring foliage, grow the plant in a sunny spot in moist but free-draining soil. If grown among spring bulbs, especially white-flowering ones with just a hint of blue, 'Aurea' will put on a strong show. By comparison, the early-summer flowers, which are white, are fairly unremarkable and just a little disappointing. On a windy site, you will need to provide a strong support to keep the plant upright.

OTHER VARIETY *V. officinalis* (larger growing, bright green leaves).

PLANT PROFILE
HEIGHT 1.5m (5ft)
SPREAD 60cm (24in)
SITE Full sun or dappled shade
SOIL Moist but free-draining
HARDINESS Fully hardy
FLOWERING Early summer

Vancouveria hexandra

V

A WOODLAND GARDEN is the perfect setting for this creeping, deciduous perennial, where it will thrive in the light shade and rich, moist but free-draining soil. A wonderful ground-cover plant, it will also do well in the shady, wilder edges of a more formal setting. Near the base of the plant the shapely leaves can reach up to 45cm (18in) long; toward the top, they gradually decrease in size to just 8cm (3in). As spring turns to summer, airy clusters of tiny white flowers appear on long leafless stems (*see inset*).

OTHER VARIETY *V. chrysantha* (smaller-growing, yellow flowers and glossy, leathery, dark green leaves; can be very invasive).

PLANT PROFILE
HEIGHT 40cm (16in)
SPREAD 40cm (16in)
SITE Partial shade
SOIL Moist but free-draining
HARDINESS Fully hardy
FLOWERING Late spring and early summer

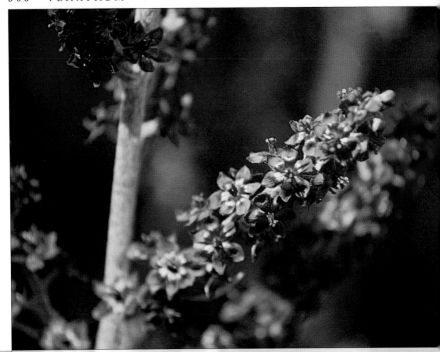

V | *Veratrum nigrum*

FROM A DENSE ROSETTE OF LONG, PLEATED LEAVES, this architectural plant sends up a tall flower stem packed with branches of tiny, dark red-brown flowers. Enjoy the effect but don't get too close because they carry an unpleasant smell. Unless you can give it a light background the intensity of the flower colour will be lost; in a gloomy setting, the green-white flowers of *Veratrum album* are more visually pleasing. All veratrums need a sheltered position with rich, moist but well-drained soil. Full sun isn't a problem, so long as you don't allow the ground to dry out. You can raise plants from seed but you will have to wait five or six years for the first flush of flowers.

OTHER VARIETY *V. viride* (a taller plant with yellowish-green flowers).

PLANT PROFILE

HEIGHT 60–120cm (24–48in)

SPREAD 60cm (24in)

SITE Partial shade

SOIL Fertile, moist but free-draining

HARDINESS Fully hardy

FLOWERING Mid- to late summer

Verbascum chaixii 'Album' **Mullein**

V

THE TALL, SHOWY SPIRES of 'Album' are dotted along their length with white, saucer-shaped flowers, each with a mauve eye. A well-loved cottage garden plant, it makes a graceful addition to the summer border. Planted in a group or drift, it looks particularly impressive against the dark background of a beech hedge. Mulleins do best in well-drained, average soil; in richer soils they will grow overly tall and require staking. There are many excellent yellow-flowering types, including the 1.2m (4ft) *Verbascum* 'Cotswold Queen' and *V.* 'Gainsborough'. For extra height, grow *V. olympicum*, at 2m (6ft), and *V. bombyciferum*, at about the same height.

OTHER VARIETY *V. chaixii* 'Pink Domino' (taller, rose-pink flowers).

PLANT PROFILE
HEIGHT 90cm (36in)
SPREAD 45cm (18in)
SITE Full sun
SOIL Average, free-draining
HARDINESS Fully hardy
FLOWERING Mid- to late summer

V | *Verbascum* 'Helen Johnson' Mullein

WITH THEIR REGAL FLOWER SPIRES, mulleins add a touch of elegance to cottage garden and border schemes. Strong yellows abound but 'Helen Johnson', a fairly recent introduction, comes in a more subtle colour that is ideal for low-key schemes. Delightful, pinkish-brown flowers, with a centre of rich purple filaments, appear from early to late summer on 45cm (18in) long branched spikes. A rosette of evergreen, grey–green, downy leaves at the base of the plant sets them off nicely. It will perform best on poor, well-drained soil in full sun; on richer soils it will grow taller and require staking.

OTHER VARIETY *V. phoeniceum* (taller-growing, white, pink, or violet to dark purple flowers).

PLANT PROFILE

HEIGHT 90cm (36in)

SPREAD 30cm (12in)

SITE Full sun

SOIL Free-draining

HARDINESS Fully hardy

FLOWERING Early to late summer

STEM CUTTING

Choose a healthy, non-flowering stem to use as a cutting. To increase the number of cuttings, divide each stem into roughly equal-size sections.

Verbena bonariensis

V

THE ULTIMATE 'SEE-THROUGH' PLANT, *Verbena bonariensis* has an open habit that can be used to great effect toward the front of a border. By thinning out some of the more dense central growth, you can further enhance the haze-like effect of the tall stems and airy flowerheads. In terms of providing valuable height, shape and colour, it is hard to beat. Free-draining soil suits it best, but it will survive in heavier ground. In colder areas, cut stems back in autumn and keep plants potted in a cool greenhouse until spring.

OTHER VARIETIES *V. corymbosa* (red-purple flowers); *V. hastata* (violet to pink flowers).

PLANT PROFILE	
HEIGHT To 2m (6ft)	
SPREAD 45cm (18in)	
SITE Full sun	
SOIL Free-draining	
HARDINESS Frost hardy	
FLOWERING Midsummer to early autumn	

V | *Vernonia noveboracensis* Ironweed

THE IMPOSING HEIGHT OF THIS PLANT makes it a useful, and very colourful, addition to the back of the border. Ironweed is topped by fluffy heads of rich red-purple or white tubular flowers. It is easy to grow and requires only moderately fertile, free-draining soil. Even though the stems are sturdy and normally self-supporting, in exposed, windy gardens staking may be necessary. These plants self-seed quite freely, so if you don't want ironweed growing all over the garden, cut off the flowers as soon as they start to fade.

OTHER VARIETY *V. crinita* (similar with red-brown flowers).

PLANT PROFILE
HEIGHT 2m (6ft)
SPREAD 60cm (24in)
SITE Full sun or partial shade
SOIL Moderately fertile, free-draining
HARDINESS Fully hardy
FLOWERING Late summer to mid-autumn

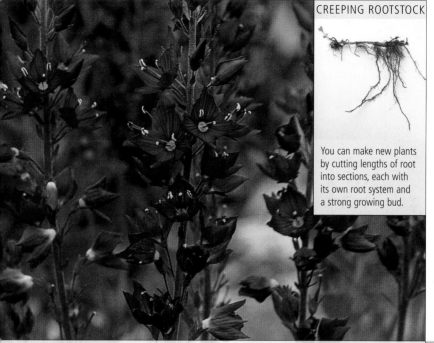

CREEPING ROOTSTOCK

You can make new plants by cutting lengths of root into sections, each with its own root system and a strong growing bud.

Veronica austriaca subsp. *teucrium* 'Crater Lake Blue' Speedwell

V

THERE ARE MANY SPEEDWELLS, all bearing candle-like spikes of saucer-shaped flowers that stand smartly erect above the foliage, but 'Crater Lake Blue' produces one of the best blues. ('Kapitän' and 'Shirley Blue' are good runners up.) Useful in formal borders and cottage gardens, it makes a wonderful sight growing in a circle around a feature plant, such as *Verbascum olympicum* with its tall spikes of yellow flowers. As the plant matures, the soft greyish-green leaves grow together to form a compact mound.

OTHER VARIETIES *V. gentianoides* 'Variegata' (blue flowers, white-variegated leaves); *V. longifolia* (larger-growing, lilac-blue flowers); *V. spicata* subsp. *incana* 'Wendy' (bright blue flowers, grey leaves).

PLANT PROFILE
HEIGHT 30cm (12in)
SPREAD 40cm (16in)
SITE Full sun or partial shade
SOIL Average, free-draining
HARDINESS Fully hardy
FLOWERING Summer

V | *Veronicastrum virginicum album* Culver's root

A CHARMING SUMMER-FLOWERING PLANT that is similar to veronica, only taller. Rising out of whorls of dark green leaves, tall, feathery, white flower spikes make it a good match with other upright plants for the back of a mixed border. It will also look imposing erupting from a carpet of rounded, lower-growing subjects. White is an extremely versatile colour and can be slotted in anywhere – among a blaze of hothouse shades or a palette of pastels. It is generally an unfussy plant but moderately fertile, moist soil is best. One drawback is that it is prone to attacks of powdery mildew.

OTHER VARIETIES *V. virginicum* 'Apollo' (light pink flowers); *V. virginicum* 'Fascination' (pale rose flowers).

PLANT PROFILE
HEIGHT 2m (6ft)
SPREAD 45cm (18in)
SITE Full sun or partial shade
SOIL Moderately fertile, moist
HARDINESS Fully hardy
FLOWERING Midsummer to early autumn

Viola riviniana Purpurea Group Common dog violet

V

TYPICALLY FOUND IN WOODLANDS, often at the base of hedgerows, the common dog violet is mostly grown as an attractive gap filler in a wild garden. It tends to be invasive and is best kept out of borders. The beautiful pale-coloured flowers, which carry a distinctive spur, can be encouraged to produce a second flush by gently trimming the plant after flowering. Like most violas, it does best in rich, moist soil. Other violas have their main flowering period during summer, when they make an excellent show among roses.

OTHER VARIETIES *V. cornuta* (smaller-growing, violet to lilac-blue flowers with white markings); *V.* 'Huntercombe Purple' (deep violet-blue flowers); *V. odorata* (fragrant, blue or white flowers).

PLANT PROFILE
HEIGHT 10–20cm (4–8in)
SPREAD 20–40cm (8–16in)
SITE Deep or partial shade
SOIL Moist, fertile
HARDINESS Fully hardy
FLOWERING Late spring and early summer

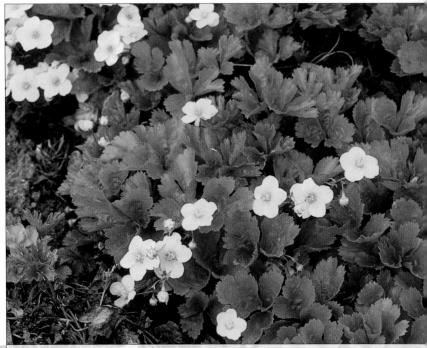

W | *Waldsteinia ternata*

THE SMALL, OPEN FLOWERS of this woodland native are set off beautifully by the contrasting dark green, semi-evergreen leaves. In dry shady areas, this quick-growing, ground cover plant will produce a welcome burst of colour at the end of spring. A woodland setting in moderately fertile, well-drained soil suits it best. Good drainage is a must and heavy, wet ground must be avoided. Given the right conditions there's a tendency for it to become invasive, so ensure it's not too close to any attractive neighbours that could get swamped. Propagating new plants by taking divisions in early spring is simple and very successful.

OTHER VARIETY *W. ternata* 'Variegata' (brighter leaves).

PLANT PROFILE

HEIGHT 10cm (4in)

SPREAD 60cm (24in)

SITE Full or partial shade

SOIL Moderately fertile, free-draining

HARDINESS Fully hardy

FLOWERING Late spring and early summer